2ⁿᵈ Chance Books

Imam Mahdi Foundation is a non-profit organization that was founded in the United Kingdom. This organization has many other projects that it manages in the UK as well as the United States. One of these initiatives that Imam Mahdi foundation has started is a program to send free books to prisoners. This program is called *2ⁿᵈ Chance Books*, which is dedicated to the descendant of the Holy Prophet (pbuh); The 11ᵗʰ Imam Hassan Al-Askari (pbuh) who spent the majority of his life in prison and under house arrest by the corrupt ruler of the time.

The incarceration rate in the USA is the highest in the world. While Americans only represent 5% of the worlds population nearly one-quarter of the entire worlds inmates have been incarcerated in the USA. The prison population in the USA is 2.3 million. Most of these prisoners will fall victim to the cycle of the revolving door and become repeat offenders if they do not have the proper resources to educate themselves properly while serving their sentences.

This program will provide the proper tools for change; Free Islamic books on belief, ethics, morality and family structure in Islam. They can use these books as a tool for self-development and to reform themselves and also their friends, loved ones and communities upon their release.

Some of the many benefits of this program are changing prisoners bad habits into good ones; achieving social reform by teaching the morals and ethics of the Holy Prophet and his Holy Household (pbut), molding leaders; producing better citizens who will be active in helping their communities upon their release, promoting awareness of the true teachings of Islam as taught by Prophet Muhammad (pbuh) and his Holy Household (pbut) and to remove misinformation and misconceptions about Islam and Muslims from the peoples minds.

This program is funded by donations to Imam Mahdi Foundation. **A donation of $25 can sponsor to send a prisoner a package of six books.** We send these books through our publishing company Yasin Publications. Please visit *www.yasinpublications.org* to donate and give the gift of knowledge to a person that could change their life and possibly the lives of everyone they interact with.

For prisoners who are reading this we want you to know that we are honored to be at your service. Please write us and let others who are interested in seeking knowledge about Islam to contact us at the address below.

Yasin Publications
Attn: 2nd Chance Books
P.O. Box 338
8253-A Backlick Rd.
Newington, VA 22122

For more information please contact
donations@yasinpublications.org

THE MYSTERY OF THE SHI'A

*CLEAR PROOFS TO ANSWER QUESTIONS REGARDING
THE BELIEFS AND PRACTICES OF SHI'A MUSLIMS*

Mateen J. Charbonneau
2/28/2008

Edited by:
Sayed Jawad Haider Syedain

***First Published in Maryland, USA
May 2013***

Paperback: 108 pages
Publisher: Yasin Publications
Date of publication: May 20, 2013
Language: English

ISBN-10: 1482686716
ISBN-13: 978-1482686715

Yasin Publications
P.O. Box 338
8253-A Backlick Rd.
Newington, VA 22122

Website: **www.yasinpublications.org**

Email: info@yasinpublications.org

IN THE NAME OF GOD, MOST BENEFICENT, MOST MERCIFUL

IMAM SADIQ (AS) SAID:
"WRITE AND SPREAD YOUR KNOWLEDGE AMONG YOUR BROTHERS. IF THE END OF YOUR LIFE APPROACHES, LEAVE YOUR BOOKS AS AN INHERITANCE FOR YOUR SONS, SINCE THERE WILL COME A TIME OF SEDITION DURING WHICH THE PEOPLE WILL ONLY FIND COMFORT WITH THEIR BOOKS."[1]

I DEDICATE THE REWARD OF THIS BOOK TO
THE COMMANDER OF THE FAITHFUL IMAM ALI
(PEACE BE UPON HIM)

---

[1] Mishkat ul Anwar by Al Tabarsi Hadith#736

About the Author

Joshua Charbonneau is an American Muslim. He was born in 1982 in Sumter, South Carolina. He is of French Canadian and American descent. He was born into a Christian family, and later chose to revert to Shi'a Islam at the age of 17, having studied both faiths. After reverting to Islam he chose the name Mateen which in Arabic means strong, firm and unshakable. His first language is English and he also learned Quranic Arabic. At age 26 he moved to Washington, DC and has been an active part of the Muslim community. He took part in a documentary by *Al-Anwar Hussain TV* entitled **Journey of the Spirit** where he narrated his incredible story on how he became a Shia Muslim.[2] In 2012 he had the opportunity to travel with the members of *Al-Anwar Hussain TV* to visit the Holy shrines of Imam Ali (as) and Imam Hussain (as) in Iraq for **Ziyarat Arbaeen**. Since March of 2013 he has been studying *Howza* (Islamic Seminary) classes under the guidance of Sheikh Mustafa Akhound at the Imam Ali Center of Springfield, VA. Mateen has also compiled and published some very in-depth books entitled **The Suffering of the Ahl ul Bayt and their Followers (Shia) throughout History**, **Christians who defended and died for Prophet Muhammad and his Family** and **Mystery of the Shia**. These titles are available at Amazon. In 2014 he co-founded a publication company entitled **Yasin Publications** and also a program to send free books to prisoners entitled **2nd Chance Books**.

---

[2] This documentary can be viewed on Youtube or www.mateenjc.com

INTRODUCTION

In the name of Allah the Most Gracious the Most Merciful. May Allah shower His blessings on our beloved Prophet Muhammad and his Purified Household. May Allah open our eyes and bestow on us the *baseera* (insight) to see the truth and an open heart to accept it. May Allah hasten the reappearance of our awaited savior, Imam Mahdi and allow us to be among his humble devoted followers. May we see the time when he will make apparent to everyone the true teachings of Islam as they were taught by his grandfather the Prophet of Allah (sawa) and not the Islam that was changed by the corrupt rulers and dictators to fit their desires. May Allah continue to bless Muhammad and the family of Muhammad and may He remove His Mercy from those who bear enmity towards them.

Then I Was Guided author, Muhammad al-Tijani al-Samawi, writes of his discovery to the true path of Islam that of adhering to the teachings of the Ahl ul bayt (as). In his book he describes what the scholar As-Sayyid As-Sadr relates to him:

As-Sayyid As-Sadr said: "It is inevitable that we pass through difficult times because the path of Ahl al-Bayt (as) is a difficult one. A man once came to see the Prophet (sawa) and said to him, 'O Messenger of Allah, I love you.' He replied, 'Then expect many tribulations.' The man said, 'I love your cousin Ali.' He replied, 'Then expect many enemies.' The man said, 'I love al-Hasan and al-Hussain.' He replied, 'Then get ready for poverty and much affliction.' What have we paid for the cause of justice for which Aba Abdillah al-Hussain (as) paid his life and the lives of his family's members and companions; and for which the Shi'a along the path of history have paid and are still paying up to the present day as a price for their allegiance to Ahl al-Bayt (as)?

My Brother, it is inevitable that we go through difficulties and give sacrifices for the cause of justice, and if Allah helped you in guiding one man to the right path, it is worth the whole world and what is within it."

Al-Tijani continues,

"As-Sayyid as-Sadr also advised me against isolating ourselves and ordered me to get even closer to my Sunni brothers whenever they wanted to keep away from me, and to consider them innocent victims of distorted history and bad propaganda, because people are the enemy of what they do not know."

This does not mean agree with their teachings, but rather not to shun them when they come to us. If we reject them when they come to us, make fun of them or are rude with them then how will they ever come towards Ahl ul Bayt (as)?

"Invite to the way of thy Lord with wisdom and beautiful preaching; and argue with them in ways that are best and most gracious: for your Lord knows, best who have strayed from His Path, and who receive guidance." (Quran 16:125)

Many Muslims have never even heard of the events that took place against the Ahl ul Bayt (as). They were taught all their lives one-way, that is all they have seen and the only path that they know. We cannot hold them accountable until we know that they are aware and then, having known, choose to reject Ahl ul Bayt (as).

The idea that prompted me to write this book was due to the fact that so many new converts to Shia Islam would always ask me why we did things differently than other sects. They would be exposed to different things upon going to various mosques. They would ask me why people pray with their hands by their sides while others would fold their arms, why was the call to prayer different, what is that "stone" we prostrate on, etc.? I used to find myself explaining these things on a daily basis, so I decided to write these questions and answers down and share them with people who came to me. That was the first phase of this project. Later on I decided to add the *Usul-e-Deen* (roots of religion) and *Furu-e-Deen* (branches of religion) being that these differ from other schools of thought as well. After I looked at what I had put together I thought that this would be a very beneficial piece of information for new converts to Islam. This was designed to help them not only to learn why Shia believe and practice the way we do, but also to learn with clear proofs from the sources. I then proceeded to add a few other chapters to help give a good basic foundation for one to start in their quest for knowledge.

In total this work deals with a variety of topics including:

- *Usul-e-Deen*
- *Furu-e-Deen*
- The Word Shia and its Meaning
- The 30 rights of a Muslim
- Forbidden acts of a Muslim
- Some Important Dates and Things to Know
- Cleanliness in Islam
- *Wudhu*
- *Salat*
- *Ahadith* showing the importance of knowing the Ahl ul Bayt (as)
- Why we say *bismillah* aloud in *salat*

- Why we say *hayya ala khayril amal* in *adhan*
- Why we dont fold our hands in *salat*
- Why we *takbir* 3 times after *salat*
- Why we dont say *as-salatu khayrum min nawm* in our *fajr adhan*
- Why we prostrate on *turbah*
- Why we say *aliyan waliyallah* in our *adhan* and *iqamah*

Note: The use of (sawa) after the Prophet's name is an Arabic abbreviation for peace be upon him and his family. The use of (AS) after the names of Fatima (AS) and the 12 Imams (AS) is an abbreviation for peace be upon him/her in Arabic; Alayhi Salam. The use of (ATF) after the name of Imam Mahdi (ATF) is an abbreviation for may Allah hasten his reappearance. The use of (RA) is an abbreviation for May Allah be pleased with him/ her in Arabic; Radi-Allahu Anhu.

TABLE OF CONTENTS

ACKNOWLEDGEMENTS

I would like to thank the following people- Sheikh Mustafa Akhound, Ibrahim Jabbar Karbalai, Hajj Mahdi Gharavi and Sayed Jawad Haider Syedain for all of their help, support, and encouragement. Thank you for motivating me to be productive and encouraging me to always continue moving forward in the path of Allah, no matter how difficult things get.

The Word Shia and its Meaning

The term Shia literally means follower. It is a term that Allah used in the Quran to refer to the followers of his Prophets. An example was Prophet Abraham (as) who was mentioned in the Quran specifically as the shia of Noah (as):

"And most surely Abraham was among the Shia of him (Noah)" *(Quran 37:83)*

Imam Ali (as) said "Allah has favored the word Shia by using it in the Holy Quran. Then verily He says 'And verily Ibrahim was one of the shia of Noah.' And you are amongst the shia of Muhammad (sawa). This name is neither restricted to a particular group nor is it a newly adopted religion." [3]

In another verse, the Quran talks about the Shia of Moses

"And he (Moses) went into the city at a time when people (of the city) were not watching, so he found therein two men fighting, one being of his shia and the other being his enemy, and the one who was of his shia cried out to him for help against the one who was of his enemy" (Quran 28:15)

Thus shia is an official word used by Allah in His Quran for His high ranking prophets as well as their followers. This is also a term that our beloved Prophet Muhammad (sawa) used for those who had love for Ali (as) and followed him as the successor after the Prophet (sawa).

The Messenger of Allah said to Ali: "Glad tidings O Ali! Verily you, your companions and your Shia (followers) will be in Paradise."

---

[3] Shia Origin and Faith" by Ayatollah Kashif al-Ghita

Sunni references:

- *Fadha'il al-Sahaba*, by Ahmad Ibn Hanbal, v2, p655
- *Hilyatul Awliyaa*, by Abu Nu'aym, v4, p329
- *Tarikh*, by al-Khateeb al-Baghdadi, v12, p289
- *al-Awsat*, by al-Tabarani
- *Majma' al-Zawa'id*, by al-Haytami, v10, pp 21-22
- al-Darqunti, who said this tradition has been transmitted via numerous authorities.
- *al-Sawa'iq al-Muhriqah*, by Ibn Hajar Haytami , Ch. 11, section 1, p247

Therefore we see the Messenger of Allah (sawa) used to say the phrase "Shia of Ali."

The Messenger of Allah (sawa) said: "The Shia of Ali are the real victorious on the day of resurrection"

Sunni references:

- *al-Manaqib Ahmad*, as mentioned in:
- *Yanabi al-Mawaddah*, by al-Qundoozi al-Hanafi, p62

The Messenger of Allah said: "O Ali! (On the day of Judgment) you and your Shia will come toward Allah well pleased and well-pleasing, and there will come to Him your enemies angry and stiff-necked (i.e., their head forced up).

Sunni references:
- *al-Tabarani*, on the authority of Imam Ali
- *al-Sawa'iq al-Muhriqah*, by Ibn Hajar al-Haythami, Ch. 11, section 1, p236

A more complete version of the tradition, which has also been reported by Sunni narrators, is as follows:

Ibn Abbas narrated: When the verse "Those who believe and do righteous deeds are the best of the creation (Quran 98:7)" was revealed, the Messenger of Allah (sawa) said to Ali: "They are you and your Shia." He continued: "O Ali! (On the day of Judgment) you and your Shia will come toward Allah well pleased and well pleasing, and your enemies will come angry with their heads forced up." Ali (as) said: "Who are my enemies?" The Prophet (sawa) replied: "He who disassociates himself from you and curses you. And glad tiding to those who reach first under the shadow of *al-'Arsh* on the day of resurrection." Ali asked: "Who are they, O the Messenger of Allah?" He replied: "Your Shia, O Ali, and those who love you."

Sunni references:

- *al-Hafidh Jamaluddin al-Dharandi*, on the authority of Ibn Abbas
- *al-Sawa'iq al-Muhriqah*, by Ibn Hajar, Ch. 11, section 1, pp 246-247

Usul-e-Deen (Roots of Religion)

Usul-e-deen means the roots of religion. Just as a tree's roots are its foundation, the religion of Allah has its foundation. These roots are the following set of 5 beliefs:

1. *Tawheed-* Oneness of Allah
2. *'Adil-* Justice of Allah
3. *Nubuwwat-* Prophet hood
4. *Imamate-* Vicegerency/Leadership
5. *Me'ad-* Resurrection

1) *Tawheed* – This is the belief in the oneness of Allah. He is without any partners. It is the belief in Him being the sole creator of the universe and all that it contains. There is nothing like Allah; nothing that can compare. We cannot give Allah human attributes; because He is above the things He has created. Allah has no image, so we cannot be created in His image as some other religions assume. He is far exalted over His creation.

We cannot see Allah and never will be able to do so. When Prophet Musa (as) asked to see Allah he replied by saying that he would never be able to see Him, *"and when Musa came to Our determined appointment and his Lord spoke to him, he said: 'My lord! Show me yourself so that I may gaze upon you.' Allah said: 'You will never[4] see Me, but gaze upon the mountain! If it stands still in its place, then you will see Me. And when his lord revealed his glory to the mountain he sent it crashing down. And Musa fell down senseless and when he woke up he said: 'Glory to you! I turn unto you repentant and I am the first of the believers."[5]*

---

[4] Here, the Qur'an uses the word *lan*: the Arabic word for "never" with an implied emphasis in the modified action's impossibility.

[5] Quran 7:143

Our intellect cannot perceive Allah. "Vision comprehends Him not but He comprehends all vision."[6] He is infinite and boundless, while we are finite and limited. Allah is not like His creation. He does not have a mate, nor does he have offspring. He is above all that the unbelievers attribute to Him.

"Say: Allah is one, Allah the eternal. He begets not, nor is He begotten. And there is nothing comparable to Him."[7]

Also some people believe that Allah is a spirit, but this is not the case as the spirits and souls are created beings of Allah as well. *"And they ask you about the spirit. Say 'the spirit is from the command of my Lord and you are not given of the knowledge except a little."[8]*

---

[6] Quran 6:103

[7] Quran 112

[8] Quran 17:85

2) *'Adil*- This is the belief in the ultimate justice and justness of Allah and that he does no injustice to anyone. He deals justly with all his creation. He will reward or punish us according to how we lived out our lives here. Did we abide and act accordingly to Allah's laws or did we discard the Quran, toss it behind our backs and live how we wanted according to our own desires?

"And we shall set up the balances of justice on the Day of Judgment so no soul will be dealt with unjustly in the least. And even if there be the weight of a grain of a mustard seed even that we will bring it into account. And sufficient are we as reckoners."[9]

"Say: Our lord will gather us together then he will judge between us with justice. And he is the greatest judge the all knowing."[10]

3) *Nubuwwat*- This is the belief in the prophet hood of all the prophets sent by Allah. When Allah wants to communicate to the people he sends messengers to teach the masses about him and his message. The way he does this is through inspiration/revelation to his chosen righteous servant of the time, so that he may be Allah's messenger and the role model for the people to follow. These messengers are called prophets, are the infallible guides of humanity. They are the way for the people to receive Allah's messages. We mold our lives according to their teachings and their character. These messengers are inspired through revelations brought by the angel Gabriel who is sent by the command of Allah. Also some were spoken to directly by Allah such as prophet Musa (as). There are 24 prophets spoken of in the Quran, but it is reported that there were as many as

---

[9] Quran 21:47

[10] Quran 34:26

124,000 prophets, Adam (as) being the first and Muhammad (sawa) being the last final messenger of Allah. There are five Major Prophets who were sent as universal prophets to all of mankind, while the other prophets were sent to particular groups or nations and sent to limited areas or specific territories. These five Major Prophets were Nuh (Noah), Ibrahim (Abraham), Musa (Moses), 'Isa (Jesus) and the seal of the prophets Muhammad, peace be upon them all.

4) *Imamate-* This is the belief in the successor ship of the 12 Imam's after the prophet hood. Since there are NO prophets after Prophet Muhammad (sawa), we have Imam's to carry on the message and to lead humanity in its course towards Allah. The Imam's have been appointed by the order of Allah for us to follow, through revelation to his last messenger Muhammad (sawa). These are the *Ulil 'Amr* (those given the authority) that Allah speaks of in Quran, 4:59. The Shi'a believe that the prophet appointed by the order of Allah 12 successors from his progeny to be the Imams for his community. The Prophet (sawa) said "After me there will be Imams from my progeny their number will be equal to the number of *Bani Isra'ils* heralds. That is 12 of whom nine will be Hussain's (as) descendants. Allah has bestowed upon all of them my knowledge and wisdom, so don't teach them because surely they know better than you. Follow them since they are definitely with the truth and the truth is with them."[11] We also believe that just as the prophets are infallible, so are the 12 imams. Allah says in Quran, 33:33

---

[11] *Peshawar Nights* by Sultanul Waizin Shirazi page 472

"Allah's wish is to remove all impurity from you O' people of the house (Ahl-ul-Bayt) and purify you with a thorough purification!"

How could Allah and his messenger appoint us guides and allow them to be sinful and corrupt? This would indeed be against Allah's justice commanding us to follow someone in sin, God forbid!

These 12 Imams are as follows:

1. Imam Ali ibn Abu Talib
2. Imam Hasan ibn Ali
3. Imam Hussain ibn Ali
4. Imam Ali Zayn-ul-'Abideen (Sajjad)
5. Imam Muhammad Baqir
6. Imam Ja'far Sadiq
7. Imam Musa Kadhim
8. Imam Ali Rida
9. Imam Muhammad Taqi (Jawad)
10. Imam Ali Naqi (Hadi)
11. Imam Hasan 'Askari
12. Imam Mahdi (May Allah hasten his reappearance)

May Allah bless them all!

5) Me'ad- Me'ad means "return." This refers to the belief in the resurrection, which takes place after the life of this world and all that is contained within it has come to an end. Allah will resurrect His creation, so that we may return before Him for judgment, before taking our place in the afterlife. On this Day of Judgment, if the person was a believer and a doer of good his place will be in *jannat* (paradise) and if he was a disbeliever and/or a mischief maker then his place will be in the hell-fire. Allah is the best of judges and He will judge us justly and according to our intentions. May He have mercy on us all! When we die, our souls will reside in *barzakh*, which is an intermediary phase between death and the resurrection, also called the life in the grave. If we were a doer of good, our grave will be a similitude to paradise and if we were evildoers, then it will be a place of punishment. When each person dies, he or she will be questioned by the two angels *Munkir* and *Nakir* about his or her beliefs. They will ask us all three major questions that we must know the answer to if we want to be granted Allah's favor:

1) Who is your Lord?
   – Allah
2) Who is your prophet?
   – Muhammad Mustafa (sawa)
3) Who is your imam?
   – Imam Mahdi (atf), who is the current Imam of our time.

May Allah allow us to all answer these questions with conviction and the certainty of strong faith!

Furu-e-Deen (Branches of Religion)

Furu-e-deen means the branches of religion. The *usul-e-deen* are the beliefs of a Muslim and the *furu-e-deen* are the practices. These branches are the obligations that Allah has commanded us to follow. These are the actions that when applied to the beliefs make us a *mu'min* (believer). If you believe without following the laws and doing the actions you will just be considered a Muslim (one who submits) and not a *mu'min*. "The wandering Arabs say: 'We believe.' Say: 'You believe not but rather say you submit for faith has not yet entered into your hearts. Yet if you obey Allah and his messenger he will not withhold from you anything of your deeds. Verily Allah is the oft forgiving the most merciful.' The true believers are those who say believe in Allah and his messenger and afterward doubt not, but strive with their wealth and their lives for the cause of Allah. Such are the sincere ones."(Quran 49:14-15). *Iman* (faith) must be accompanied with actions. These branches of religion are ten, which are:

1) *Salat* - Prayer
2) *Saum* - Fasting
3) Hajj- Pilgrimage
4) *Zakat*- consists of the payment of a portion of certain assets for the cause of Allah.
5) *Khums*- consists of 20% of ones income that is given for the cause of Allah.
6) *Jihad*- Striving/Fighting in the cause of Allah with your wealth, property, and selves
7) *Amr bil ma'ruf*- Enjoining what is right
8) *Nahi 'anil munkar*- Forbidding what is wrong
9) *Tawalli*- Love for Allah, the prophet (sawa), the prophets family (as), and their friends
10) *Tabarri*- Disassociation from the enemies of Allah, those who hate the prophet (sawa), hate the prophets family (as) and hate their friends.

Salat- These are the five daily prayers that all Muslims are obligated to make. This is our direct line of communication to Allah. By staying in the remembrance of Allah we will refrain from shameful deeds.

"Recite that which has been revealed to you of the Book and keep up prayer; surely prayer keeps (one) away from indecency and evil, and certainly the remembrance of Allah is the greatest, and Allah knows what you do."[12]

These 5 prayers are as follows:

1) *Fajr*- the dawn prayer
2) *Zuhr*- the noon prayer
3) *Asr*- the afternoon prayer
4) *Maghrib*- the after sunset prayer
5) *Isha*- the evening prayer

The Prophet (sawa) said that on the Day of Judgment the first thing that we are going to be asked about by Allah is the *salat*. If the prayers are accepted then all other deeds will be accepted but if the prayers weren't accepted then all the other deeds will be rejected.

So dear brothers and sisters lets please guard our *salat* and be punctual in performing them.

---

[12] Quran 29:45

Saum- This is the fasting in the month of Ramadan, the 9th month of the Islamic calendar. This is the month that the Quran was revealed to our beloved Prophet (sawa). Also all the other books of Allah were revealed in this month as well to their respected prophets (as). Fasting is made for us to obtain piety (*taqwa*). It is reported that fasting is a shield against the hell-fire. We also give up the luxuries of life and thus see how it is for the people who do without. This will make us more compassionate towards mankind, especially those who are less fortunate. We abstain from eating, drinking, sexual intercourse, vain talk, etc. from dawn till after sunset. This is a good time to work on ourselves and give up our bad habits and start fresh, *inshallah* (God-willing). Blessings are also increased during this blessed month for the good deeds. Traditions state that if you complete the month of fasting successfully all of your sins will be forgiven. May Allah grant us all this great mercy!

Hajj- This is the pilgrimage to the holy city of Makkah (Mecca) to visit and fulfill the rituals at the Holy *Kabah*. The *Kabah* is the house of worship that prophet Ibrahim (as) and his son Isma'eel (as) built. This trip to Makkah (Mecca) is obligatory upon the Muslim only once in his life if you have the means to do so, otherwise it is not held against you. We should all have the *niyyat* (intention) in our heart to make Hajj, so that even if we die not being able to do so then may Allah reward us for our intentions, *Insha Allah* (God willing).

"In it are clear signs, the standing place of Ibrahim, and whoever enters it shall be secure, and pilgrimage to the House is incumbent upon men for the sake of Allah, (upon) every one who is able to undertake the journey to it; and whoever disbelieves, then surely Allah is Self-sufficient, above any need of the worlds."[13]

---

[13] Quran 3:97

Zakat- The Arabic word zakat means to purify. This charity is a way to purify our wealth. *Zakat* consists of the payment of a portion of certain assets for the cause of Allah.

From what things should *zakat* be paid?

1. The three groups of grazing livestock: cows, sheep and goats and camels.

2. The four types of grains: dates, raisins, wheat and barley.

3. Two types of coinage: gold and silver.

Thus, *zakat* has to be paid obligatorily from nine things. It is recommended that *zakat* should also be paid from other things like properties and business assets.

To whom should *zakat* be given?

Zakat should be expended in eight categories:
1. The poor.
2. The penurious: one whose condition is more severe than that of a poor person.
3. Officials who are appointed to collect the zakat.
4. Matters that may be considered to be for the cause of God, that is anything that is for the benefit of the Muslims, be it related to his religious or worldly affairs.
5. Debtors who are unable to pay their debts.
6. Wayfarers who cannot travel any further and cannot afford to return to their own homeland.
7. Those who receive from the zakat in order either to strengthen the faith already present in their hearts or to discourage them from harming the Muslims.
8. Slaves: bonds persons who live under difficult conditions should be purchased with zakat money or freed.

Khums- This is the 20% of ones income that is given for the cause of Allah.

"And know that whatever thing you gain, a fifth of it is for Allah and for the Messenger and for the near of kin and the orphans and the needy and the wayfarer, if you believe in Allah and in that which We revealed to Our servant, on the day of distinction, the day on which the two parties met; and Allah has power over all things."[14]

From what income should *khums* be given?

From seven things:
1. Treasure from war.
2. Things that have been acquired by means of diving in the seas.
3. Mineral ore.
4. Profits and gains.
5. Land that a non-Muslim buys from a Muslim.
6. A *halal* (lawful or religiously permissible) gain that has been mixed with a *haram* (unlawful or religiously forbidden) gain.
7. Treasure.

To whom should *khums* be paid?

A part of the *khums* should be paid to the Muslim jurist so that he may expend it according to Islamic activities as seems fit to him. The person concerned expends the remainder for helping orphans, poor people and needy travellers, from among the descendants of the Prophet (sawa).

---

[14] Quran 8:41

Jihad- The Arabic word jihad means to strive. Jihad is generally divided into two forms: the greater jihad and the lesser jihad.

The greater jihad is an internal struggle to be pious and good. The Prophet (sawa) is reported to have said: "The greatest jihad is the jihad against your own evil desires." It is incumbent upon us to strive in the cause of Allah to better our surroundings and ourselves.

The lesser jihad is an external struggle, or defense, in protection of Islam and Muslims. It is obligatory for us to defend our religion when it is in danger, but we should never be the aggressors.

Let us take a look at what the Quran says about the severity of killing a person unjustly.

"Whosoever kills a human being for other than manslaughter or corruption in the earth, it shall be as if he had killed all mankind, and whoever saves the life of one, it shall be as if he had saved the life of all mankind."[15]

Let us also look at this hadith related by Imam al-Sadiq (as) about the rules and precautions of war

"The Messenger of Allah (sawa), when he wanted to send out troops, called them and bid them to sit before him. He then said to them: Go out in the name of Allah and by Allah and in the way of Allah and according to the religion of the Messenger of Allah. Do not handcuff or tie up (the prisoners of war), do not mutilate (even the dead), and do not betray people. Do not kill the old man, the child or the woman, and do not cut down a single tree except when you are forced to do so. And if any

---

[15] Quran 5:32

Muslim be he lofty or lowly gives a man of the Polytheists sanctuary, then his safety must be secured so that he hears the word of Allah. If he follows you then he is your brother in religion. If he refuses then give him his sanctuary and seek the help of Allah regarding him."[16]

Allah says in the Noble Quran *"And if any one of the polytheists seeks your protection, then grant him protection so that he may hear the words of Allah. Then deliver him to his place of safety. That is because they are a people who do not know."[17]*

War, Peace and Non-Violence author, Ayatollah Sayed Muhammad Shirazi, writes of the Prophet's peaceful methods:

The Messenger of Allah, Muhammad (sawa), progressed, as we have said, through peace that he adopted as his formula. One example of this is Mecca, the capital of unbelief and idolatry and the capital of waging war against the Messenger of Allah (sawa). The people of Mecca confronted the Messenger of Allah by every possible means. They banished him, killed his (foster) daughter Zaynab, confiscated his wealth and killed many of his followers. Finally they tried to assassinate him so he fled secretly to Madina but they continued their plots against his holy mission. Despite this, after more than twenty years, when the Messenger (sawa) wanted to conquer Mecca, he made preparations then proceeded to conquer that city peacefully without one drop of blood being spilt. Among the preparations he made were when he took possession of Khaibar, he took as spoils a large hoard of golden vessels as many as twenty thousand in number and of differing sizes. The Messenger (sawa) sent a number of these vessels to be shared out amongst the poor

---

[16] *War, Peace and Non-Violence* by Ayatollah Sayed Muhammad Shirazi page 21

[17] Quran 9:6

of Mecca even though they were unbelievers, polytheists, and warring against the Messenger of Allah (sawa). When these golden vessels arrived for the people of Mecca, they were confused and amazed. They said: 'We fight this man, we confiscate his property, we kill his followers and his relatives and he deals with us in such a kind manner.'

This was an overture from the Messenger of Allah (sawa) to bring Islam to Mecca and to destroy the idols and to establish peace between the people. When the Messenger of Allah (sawa) conquered Mecca, Abu Sufyan, his archenemy came and the Messenger of Allah (sawa) pardoned him. Not only this but he made his house a sanctuary saying: 'Whoever enters the house of Abu Sufyan is safe.' Then he turned to, the wife of Abu Sufyan, Hind the woman famous for her immoral acts and attacks on the Messenger of Allah (sawa). She who had torn open the abdomen of Master of the Martyrs Hamza, and amputated his ears and his nose and mutilated him in the vilest manner, taking out his liver and chewing it in her mouth. This woman, this 'war criminal' was sent by the Messenger of Allah a document of pardon. By this, the Messenger of Allah (sawa) recorded the most magnificent example in the history of creation of forgiveness even of his most ardent enemies.

The chroniclers report that Mecca at this time was the capital of unbelief and Polytheism, hypocrisy, selfishness and pride. When it surrendered to the Messenger of Allah (sawa), most of the people did not announce their entry into Islam but rather remained on the way of Polytheism. The Messenger of Allah (sawa) did not coerce them to accept Islam ever but instead left them to themselves so that they would live by themselves under the rule of Islam to enter Islam in the future.[18]

---

[18] *War, Peace and Non-Violence* by Ayatollah Sayed Muhammad Shirazi pages 70-71

As the Quran states *"There shall be no compulsion in [acceptance of] the religion."[19]*

So as we can see, our Holy Prophet (sawa) and his family were never the aggressors. They defended their religion by performing *Jihad* when they were attacked, but they would always strive to resolve matters peacefully. When forced to perform *Jihad* there were very strict rules and regulations to insure that the Muslims did not over step the boundaries.

Amr bil ma'ruf- This means enjoining what is right; inviting others to piety and righteousness. This should be done upon yourself first, then your family, then upon the people in your surroundings. This is done with the intention to prevent a corrupt society. If we constantly remind one another to do good deeds then we will stay conscience of Allah, and thus will stay on the straight path.

"You are the best nation produced [as an example] for mankind. You enjoin what is right and forbid what is wrong and believe in Allah. If only the People of the Scripture had believed, it would have been better for them. Among them are believers, but most of them are defiantly disobedient."[20]

Nahi 'anil munkar- This means forbidding what is wrong; advising and admonishing against *haraam* and forbidden acts. This goes along with the above obligation. If we see someone doing wrong and going astray then we should admonish that person. This way, he will remember Allah and seek his forgiveness. And refrain from the act of disobedience.

---

[19] Quran 2:256

[20] Quran 3:110

Tawalli- This is the love that we must cultivate in our hearts for the Messenger of Allah (sawa) his family (as), and their followers. We must have love for these people, as they are the near and dear ones to Allah. They are our role models, and our guides for this life.

Allah commands us to love them in the Quran.

"Say: I do not ask of you any reward for it but love for my near relatives (Ahl ul Bayt); and whoever earns good, We give him more of good therein; surely Allah is Forgiving, Grateful."[21]

Allah loves these individuals so we should also show our love for them. The Prophet (sawa) is reported to have said: "None of you truly believes until he loves me more than he loves his own family." If it were not for them then we would still be in the realm of ignorance and misguidance. We should love them for showing us the truth, how to apply it to our daily lives and for all of the great sacrifices they made to preserve the religion! Praise be to Allah who made perfect His religion and completed His favor with the establishment of the commander of the faithful, Ali ibn Abi Talib's (as) love and authority! Praise be to Allah who blessed us to be among those who cling and hold to the love and authority of the commander of the faithful and all of the Imam's, peace be upon them all!

Tabarri- This is the disassociation that we have from the enemies of Allah, enemies of His Prophet (sawa), enemies of the Prophet's family (as) and their followers. Islam teaches us to love for the sake of Allah and also to disassociate for the sake of Allah. Allah says in the Quran

"Allah has not made for any man two hearts within him."[22]

---

[21] Quran 42:23

[22] Quran 33:4

So love for Allah *and* for His enemy can never co-exist in the heart of a true believer. We must disassociate ourselves from these people and their corrupt ideologies. Just think of it rationally, who would want to associate and be around someone who was hostile to Islam and hated your way of life? "And [mention, O Muhammad], when Abraham said to his father (caretaker) and his people, *'Indeed, I am disassociated (baree) from that which you worship. Except for He who created me; and indeed, He will guide me.' And he made it a word remaining among his descendants that they might return [to it].* [23]

Remember, that Allah also says in the Quran that if a person, irrespective of their faith, is not hostile to Islam then we should treat them justly.

"Allah does not forbid you respecting those who have not made war against you on account of (your) religion, and have not driven you forth from your homes, that you show them kindness and deal with them justly; surely Allah loves the doers of justice. Allah only forbids you respecting those who made war upon you on account of (your) religion, and drove you forth from your homes and backed up (others) in your expulsion, that you make friends with them, and whoever makes friends with them, these are the unjust." [24]

---

[23] Quran 43:26-28

[24] Quran 60:8-9

A Muslim's Rights

The Prophet (sawa) said: "Every believer has 30 obligations over his brother-in-faith which could not be said to have been met unless he either performs them or is excused from performing them by his brother-in-faith."[25]

1. Forgiving his mistakes
2. Being merciful and kind to him when he is in a foreign land
3. Guarding his secrets
4. Giving him a hand when he is about to fall
5. Accepting his apology
6. Discouraging backbiting about him
7. Persisting in giving him good advice
8. Treasuring his friendship
9. Fulfilling his trust
10. Visiting him when he is ill
11. Being with him at his death
12. Accepting his invitations and presents
13. Returning his favors in the same way
14. Thanking him for his favors
15. Being grateful for his assistance
16. Protecting his honor and property
17. Helping him meet his needs
18. Making an effort to solve his problems
19. Saying to him *Yarhamuka Allah* (May Allah have mercy on you) when he sneezes
20. Guiding him to the thing he has lost
21. Answering his greeting
22. Taking him at his word
23. Accepting his bestowals

---

[25] Jami al-Sa'adat (The Collector of Felicities) by Muhammad Mahdi ibn Abi Zarr al-Naraqi pg 37-38 published by Yasin Publications

24. Confirming him if he swears to something
25. Being kind and friendly towards him
26. Helping him when he is unjust by stopping him or when he is being a victim of injustice
27. Not being unsympathetic and hostile towards him
28. Refraining from feeling bored and fed up of him
29. Not forsaking him in the midst of troubles
30. Liking for him whatever good you would like for yourself, and disliking for him whatever you would dislike for yourself.

These are the morals we should live by and the way that we should treat each other. Just imagine if we lived by all of these how much better this world would be. The Prophet (sawa) gave us the remedy for our social problems, but it is up to us to put them into practice.

Forbidden Acts of a Muslim

"And if you avoid the greater sins which you are forbidden We will expiate from you your smaller misdeeds and We will admit you an honorable entry."[26]

The 8th Imam, Ali Ar-Rida (as), wrote a letter prohibiting the following sinful acts, as they were greater sins[27]:

1. Killing those whose murder is prohibited by Allah
2. Adultery
3. Stealing
4. Drinking wine
5. Disobeying one's parents
6. Fleeing the battle field (desertion)
7. Stealing the property of orphans
8. Eating animals found already dead, animals not slaughtered in the name of Allah, blood, and pigs (This prohibition stands unless you are compelled)
9. Accepting usury when it is obvious
10. Consuming prohibited wealth
11. Gambling
12. Cheating in business by under-measuring
13. Accusing chaste women of adultery
14. Homosexuality
15. Despair towards (and losing hope in) the mercy of Allah
16. Not fearing the divine retribution
17. Not acknowledging the bounties of Allah
18. Co-operating with the oppressors
19. Associating with the oppressors
20. Taking a false oath

---

[26] Quran 4:31

[27] Greater Sins by Ayatollah Dastaghayb

21. Obstructing the rights of someone without any valid reason
22. Lying
23. Pride
24. Wasting wealth
25. Spending in ways not permitted by Allah
26. Betraying the trust of others
27. Considering *hajj* of the Holy *Kabah* unimportant
28. Fighting the friends of Allah
29. Enjoying vain pre-occupations
30. Persisting in committing sins

Some Important Dates and Things to Know

- When was the Prophet (sawa) born?

  17th of *Rabbi Al-Awwal* 570 AD

- Where?

  Makkah (Mecca)
- Who were his parents and close family members?

  Father- 'Abdullah ibn 'Abdul Muttalib who died before his birth

  Mother- Aminah bint Wahhab who died when the Prophet was 6

  Grandfather- 'Abdul Muttalib who died when the Prophet was 8

  Uncle- Abu Talib who died in the year 620 AD

- When did the Prophet (sawa) marry?

  595 AD when he was 25 years old

- To whom?

  Khadijah bint Khuwaylid, she was also 25 years old[28]

---

[28] In his book, *The Prophet Muhammad: A Mercy to the World*, Ayatollah Sayed Muhammad Shirazi states that Khadija was 25 years old. Some other historians have different views about Khadija's age. Some say that she was 40 years old and also some say 28 years old.

- When was Ali ibn Abu Talib born?

  600 AD

- Where?

  Inside the Holy *Kabah*[29]

- Who were Ali's parents?

  Father- Abu Talib

  Mother- Fatimah bint Asad

- Did the prophet Muhammad (sawa) and Khadijah have any children?

  Yes. Two boys named Qasim and Abdullah who each died at a young age, and one daughter Fatimah (as). The other girls that people attribute to being their daughters were actually the daughters of Khadijah's sister, who died. Khadijah took care of them so they were the Prophet's foster daughters.

- Did the prophet Muhammad (sawa) have any other children during his life?

  Yes, a son named Ibrahim who also died at a young age. Ibrahim was born from the Prophets wife, Mary the Copt.

---

[29] Imam Ali was the only person in history to ever be born inside of the Holy *Kabah*.

- When did the first revelation come down?

  27th of Rajab 610 AD at the age of 40.

- Where?

  In the cave of Hira in Mount *Noor*, in Northeast Makkah.

- What was the first revelation?

  Surah 96 ayats 1-5

- When was the Quran revealed in its entirety?

  In the month of Ramadan on the Night of Power[30]

- When did the Prophet (sawa) emigrate?

  622 AD

- Where to?

  Madina

- Why?

  Too much oppression from the idolaters and Allah commanded him to leave

---

[30] The Quran was revealed in its complete form on the night of power and also gradualy over the course of 23 years.

- Whom did Fatimah marry?

  Ali ibn Abu Talib

- When?

  624 AD

- Did they have children?

  Yes, two boys Hassan & Hussain and two girls Zaynab & Umm Kulthum.

- What were the major battles fought in Islam?

  Badr in 624 AD against the idolaters
  Uhud in 625 AD against the idolaters
  Khandaq in 627 AD against the idolaters and the Jews
  Khaybar in 628 AD against the Jews
  Hunayn in 630 AD against the idolaters

- When was the Prophet murdered?

  632 AD at the age of 63

- Where?

  Madina

- How?

  He was martyred by poison

- What is the year of grief?

  The year 620 AD when Khadijah and Abu Talib were martyred due to the hardships they suffered during the exile.

- When was Imam Ali (as) murdered?

  21st of *Ramadan* at the age of 63 in the year 40 AH which coincides to the year 661 AD

- How?

  Struck by a poisoned sword to the head while he was prostrating to Allah during his *Fajr salat* (morning prayers) on the 19th of *Ramadan*

- By whom?

  Abdur Rahman ibn Muljim

- Amongst some of the first people to accept Islam were Ali bin Abu Talib, Khadija, Zayd ibn Haritha, Abu Talib, his wife Fatimah bint Asad, their son Jafar ibn Abu Talib, Abu Thar, Ammar Yasir and his family.

Cleanliness in Islam

The Holy Prophet (sawa) said: "Try to be clean as much as you are able to. Verily, Allah has based the foundation of Islam on cleanliness; hence, never can a person enter Paradise but the clean ones."[31]

Imam Musa Kadhim (as) said:

There are five traditions about the head and five others related to the body. The first five concerning the head are:
1. Rinsing the mouth
2. Trimming the mustache
3. Combing the hair
4. Rinsing the nostrils
5. Letting the beard grow

The second five concerning the body are;
1. Circumcision
2. Shaving the pubic hair
3. Depilating the arm-pit hair
4. Clipping the nails
5. Cleansing the private parts (after using the rest-room)"[32]

All this is done for cleanliness. For example, shaving the armpits is good for keeping down odor, since the hair traps in odors. Clipping the nails removes dirt from under them. Shaving the pubic hairs keeps down odor and also allows you to keep yourself clean. We have to be clean when we stand before our Lord in prayer. These aspects deal with the physical purification, which is the first level of purifying oneself

---

[31] *Kanz-ul-'Ummal, Tradition 26002*

[32] From the book Khisal by Saduq page 125

Wudhu (Ablution) and Tayammum (Ablution in the absence of water)

"O Believers! When you prepare for prayers, wash your faces and your hands up to the elbows, and wipe your heads, and your feet to the ankles ... and [if you] do not find water then betake yourselves to clean earth and wipe your faces and your hands with it."[33]

Prior to performing the daily prayers, and as a recommended or obligatory prerequisite to other acts of worship, Muslims must purify themselves—this is usually done with water. The minor form of this purification with water is called *Wudhu*, while the major form is called *Ghusl*. If water is not available, the purification can be performed with clean earth or soil, and is called *Tayammum*.

When to Perform *Wudhu*

Every Muslim must be in a state of spiritual purification before performing the daily obligatory prayers. The same state of purification must also be achieved before numerous other acts of worship such as optional prayers, touching the script of the Qur'an, and the rites of the pilgrimage (Hajj). In most cases, it is sufficient to perform *Wudhu* in order to achieve this purification. However, at other times, a *Ghusl* must be performed. Please note that *Ghusl* (Full Wash) is not covered in this book.

---

[33] Qur'an: Chapter 5, Verse 6

How to Perform *Wudhu*

Niyyat: Make your intention as, "I am performing *Wudhu* for the pleasure of Allah, and to seek closeness to Him".

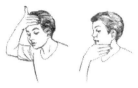

Washing the face: First, remove anything on the face (and hands) that may prevent water from reaching the skin before beginning *Wudhu* (physical items such as a watch, ring, make-up, etc... or even things such as paint or anything which would act as a barrier over the skin). Take a handful of water in the right hand and pour this water over the face from the top (just above the forehead). Then, using the right hand, wipe the face from the tip of where the hairline is to the bottom of the chin such that the water reaches all parts from the hairline to chin, and the entire horizontal plane of the face within the reach of the span of the hand from the middle finger to the thumb. To ensure that all external parts have been washed, include a bit of the inner parts of your nose, lips, and eyes in the washing. You do not, however, need to wash the complete inner portion of these parts. Washing once as described above is obligatory. A second such washing is recommended while subsequent washings are prohibited.

Washing the arms: Using the left hand, pour water over the right arm from the elbow to the fingertips and then, with the same hand, wipe the water over both sides of the arm to ensure that all parts are washed. Then do the same for the left arm by using the right hand. The washing must be done from the elbows to the fingertips and not vice versa. Pour water from a little above the elbow to ensure that the whole forearm is covered.

Wash in such a way that the water penetrates the hair, if any, and reaches the skin. Again, washing once as described above is obligatory. A second such washing is recommended while subsequent washings are prohibited.

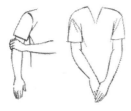

Regarding washing of the face and hands:
Wash by pouring water from top to the bottom. Washing the other way will invalidate your *Wudhu*. In general, wash a little beyond the required limit in order to make sure all parts are covered.

Wiping the head: Next, wipe the front most quarter of the head with the moisture that remains in your right hand. Wipe from the upper part of the head downwards (from the back of the head towards the face). It is recommended to wipe the length of at least one finger. When wiping the front most quarter of the head it is recommended to use three fingers together (the middle finger, index finger and ring finger). While wiping the head, your hand should not touch your forehead. Doing otherwise will cause the water of the forehead to mix with the wetness of your hand, and this will render the act of wiping your right foot invalid, since the act of wiping must be done with the wetness of the hands only.

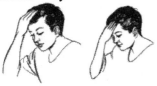

Wiping the feet: Finally, wipe your feet with the moisture that remains in your hands. Wipe starting from the tip of the toes up till the ankle joint. Wipe your right foot with your right hand first, and 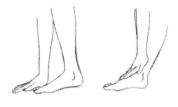 then your left foot with your left hand. Perform this for each foot only once. It is better to wipe at least the width of three joined fingers (the middle finger, index finger and ring finger), and better yet to wipe your entire foot with your entire hand. At the time of wiping the foot, actually pull the hand from toes to the ankle joint (as described above) along the length of the toe-tips till the ankles. Do not just place your whole hand on your foot and pull up a little. Please note that wiping of the feet performed on socks or shoes are not valid.

Regarding wiping of the head and feet:
While wiping your head and feet, move your hand over them. Keeping your hand stationary and moving your feet / head under your hand will invalidate your *Wudhu*. However, there is no harm if your head and feet move slightly during the wiping. The parts you are wiping must be dry before you begin wiping, and if they are so wet that the moisture on your palm has no effect on them, the wiping will be void. Slight dampness on the part you are wiping is permissible as long as the moisture of the palm is immediately mixed with it when wiping.

Wiping **must** be done with the moisture remaining on the palms after washing. Do not re-wet your hands with new water. In the case where the palms become dry before wiping, the palms can be re-wet with water from the beard, moustache, eyebrows, or the other organs of *Wudhu*.

When to Perform *Tayammum*

Perform *Tayammum* in place of *Wudhu* or *Ghusl* when:

- Not enough water is available for *Wudhu* or *Ghusl*.
- Obtaining water for *Wudhu* will endanger your life or property or you are unable to procure water by any means.
- Using the available water will leave insufficient water for drinking and pose a risk of thirst, illness, death or difficulty for yourself or your dependents.
- Washing your face and hands with water will endanger your health.
- Water is available but you do not have permission to use it.
- There is a risk that performing *Wudhu* or *Ghusl* will cause the time of the entire or a part of the prayer to end.
- If the body or clothing is ritually impure (*najis*) and the person possesses only as much water so that if he was to perform *Wudhu* or *Ghusl*, no more water would be available for making his body or clothing pure for prayer.

How to Perform *Tayammum*

Niyyat: Make your intention as, "I am doing *Tayammum* in place of *Wudhu* (or *Ghusl*), for the pleasure of Allah and to seek closeness to Him."

Step 1: Strike the palms of both hands simultaneously on earth, sand, or stone (in order of preference) which is dry and clean. (See **Figure 1**).

Step 2: Pull both palms together from the beginning of the forehead where the hair grows down to the bridge of the nose. Both sides of the forehead joining the ears and over the eyebrows should be included. (See **Figures 2 and 3**)

Step 3: Then pull the left palm on the whole back of the right hand from the wrist bone to the fingertips. (See **Figure 4**)

Step 4: Then pull the right palm on the whole back of the left hand.
Step 5: Strike the palms together upon a valid surface a second time as in Step 1.
Step 6: Repeat Step 3.
Step 7: Repeat Step 4.

Figure 1   **Figure 2**   **Figure 3**   **Figure 4**

Adhan (Call to Prayer) and *Iqamah*

Recital	Transliteration	Translation
4x	Allahu Akbar	Allah is the Greatest
2x	Ash-hadu anlā ilāha illallāh	I bear witness that there is no God except Allah
2x	Ash-hadu anna Muhammadar rasūlullāh	I bear witness that Muhammad is the Messenger of Allah
2x	Ash-hadu anna Aliy-yan waliy-yullah *	I testify that Ali is the vicegerent of Allah
2x	Hayya 'alas-salāt	Make haste towards prayer
2x	Hayya 'alal-falāh	Make haste towards success
2x	Hayya 'alā Khairil-'amal	Make haste towards the best of deeds
2x	Allahu Akbar	Allah is the Greatest
2x	Lā ilāha illallāh	There is no god except Allah

According to the ruling of Ayatollah Sayed Sadiq Shirazi saying this is wajib (obligatory) in adhan and iqama. He states, "Evidently the phrase 'Ash-hadu anna Aliy-yan waliy-yullah' is the integral part of both adhan and iqamah, as some narrations point to that." (Islamic Laws by Ayatollah Sayed Sadiq Shirazi page 135)

Some of the other Shi'a scholars say that this phrase is not an integral part of Adhan and Iqamah, but that it is recommended (Mustahab).

Iqama:

"Allah is the greatest" (twice)	Allāhu akbar
"I bear witness that there is no god except Allah" (twice)	Ash'hadu an lā 'ilaha 'illāl-lāh
"I bear witness that Muhammad is the Messenger of Allah" (twice)	Ash'hadu anna Muhammadar-rasūlul-lāh
"I bear witness that Ali is the vicegerent of God" (twice)	Ash-hadu anna Aliy-yan waliy-yullah'
"Make haste towards prayer" (twice)	Hayya `alāŝ-ŝalāt
"Make haste towards success" (twice)	Hayya `alāl-falāĥ
"Make haste towards the best of deeds" (twice)	Hayya `alā khaīril-'amal'
"Prayer has begun" (twice)	*Qad qāmatis-salaat*
"Allah is the greatest" (twice)	Allāhu akbar
"There is no god except Allah" (once)	Lā 'ilaha 'illāl-lāh

The majority of scholars state that it is mustahab for a man or a woman to perform the adhan and iqamah before the daily obligatory salah, rather the iqamah should not be neglected. It is mandatory to perform the iqamah after the adhan, and it is not valid to perform it before the adhan.

Salat (Prayer)

"...but when ye are free from danger, set up Regular Prayers: For such Prayers are enjoined on believers at stated times."[34]

---

[34] Quran 4 :103

The Five Daily Prayers

Muslims are commanded to perform five prayers per day. These prayers are obligatory on every Muslim above the age of puberty, with the exception being those who are mentally ill, menstruating, or experiencing post-partum bleeding. Those who are ill or otherwise physically unable to offer their prayers in the traditional form are permitted to offer their prayers while sitting or lying, as they are able.

The five prayers are all given certain prescribed times in which they must be performed, unless there is a compelling reason for not being able to perform them on time. Some Muslims offer voluntary prayers immediately before and after the prescribed *wajib* (obligatory) prayers. The number of *raka'ah* for each of the five obligatory prayers as well as the voluntary prayers (before and after) are listed below:

Name	Prescribed time period	Recitation of wajib salat	Voluntary before wajib	Wajib (obligatory)	Voluntary after wajib
Fajr	Dawn to sunrise	Audible	2 Raka'ah	2 Raka'ah	-
Dhuhr	After true noon until Asr	In a low voice, except for Bismillah**	8 Raka'ah in sets of 2	4 Raka'ah	-
Asr	See note*	In a low voice, except for Bismillah**	8 Raka'ah in sets of 2	4 Raka'ah	-
Maghrib	After sunset until dusk	Audible		3 Raka'ah	4 Raka'ah in sets of 2
Isha	See note*	Audible		4 Raka'ah	2 Raka'ah (sitting)

Note: According to Shia Muslims, 'Asr prayer and 'Ishaa prayer have no set times but are performed from mid-day. Zuhr and 'Asr prayers must be performed before sunset, and the time for 'Asr prayer starts after Zuhr has been performed. Maghrib and 'Ishaa prayers must be performed before midnight, and the time for 'Ishaa prayer can start after Maghrib has been performed, as long as no more light remains in the western sky signifying the arrival of the true night.

** What is meant by reciting aloud is that the minimum level of your voice can be heard by others nearby, whereas the minimum level for reciting in a low voice is that the person reciting is able to hear it himself.[35]

Preparation:
Stand upright facing the *Qiblah* (direction of Mecca) and recite the *adhan* and *iqama*. Please note that all the recitations during the prayer must be in Arabic. Although approximate transliteration has been given below for each recitation, it is best to try and learn the Arabic script and pronunciations.

Niyyat: Form the following solemn intention in your mind: **"I offer this ____** (name of a particular prayer) **prayer, of ____** (number of units) *rak`ah*'s **seeking closeness to God".**

The First *Rak`ah*:

Takbirat ul Ihram: Lift both hands up to the ears palms facing forward and say: *Allaahu akbar*
God is the greatest

This sentence, the ***Takbir***, will be repeated several times during the prayer.

---

[35] Refer to Shara'l al-Islam Vol. 1 pg. 83 Ch. Kitab as-Salat Section Qirah

Qiyam (standing): Remain in the standing position with arms by the side while performing the recitations in the next step, *Qira'ah*.

Ayatollah Sayed Sadiq Shirazi states to hold (takkatuf), which is to place the hands over one another across the body during salat invalidates the prayer. (Islamic Laws by Ayatollah Sayed Sadiq Shirazi page 158

Ayatollah Sayed Sistani states if a person folds his hands as a mark of humility and reverence, his prayers will be void, but this is based on precautionary rule. However, there is no doubt about it being haram (forbidden) if it is done believing that shariah *ordains it. There is no harm if a person places one hand on another forgetfully, or due to helplessness, or* taqiyyah *(hiding ones faith due to fear for his life), or for some other purposes, like, scratching. (Islamic Laws by Ayatollah Sayed Sistani #1138 and 1139)*

Qira'ah (recitation): Initially, recite silently:

"A'udhu billahi min nash shaytan nir rajeem

(I seek refuge in Allah from the cursed satan)"

Then recite the first Chapter of the Holy Qur'an, *Surat al-Fatiha.*

In the first and second *rakats* of *Zuhr* and *Asr* prayers one should say Bismillah loudly. It is *mustahab* (recommended) also to recite *Surah al-Hamd* and other *Surah* distinctly, with a pause at the end of every verse (i.e. not joining it with the next verse), and while reciting *Surah al-Hamd* and *Surah*, one should pay attention to the meanings of each verse.

1. **Bismillaahir-Rahmanir-Raheem**	1. In the Name of God, the Merciful, the Compassionate
2. **Al-hamdu lillaahi rabbil-'alameen**	2. Praise belongs to God, Lord of the Worlds,
3. **Ar-rahmanir raheem**	3. the Merciful, the Compassionate,
4. **Maliki yawmid-deen**	4. Master of the Day of Judgment;
5. **Iyyaka na'abudu wa iyyaka nasta`een**	5. We worship only You, and from You alone do we seek help.
6. **Ihdinas-sirat al-mustaqeem**	6. Lead us on the straight path,
7. **sirat al-ladheena an`amta `alayhim ghayril maghdubi `alayhim wa la'd-daalleen**	7. The path of those whom You have blessed, not of those on whom is [Your] Wrath, nor of those who have gone astray.

Ayatollah Sayed Sadiq Shirazi states to say "amin" (amen) after reciting al-Hamd invalidates one's prayer. However, if one says this inadvertently, or on grounds of taqiyyah, to hide his faith and protect himself in dangerous surrounding, his salah is not rendered void. (Islamic Laws by Ayatollah Sayed Sadiq Shirazi page 158)

Ayatollah Sayed Sistani states that something that invalidates prayers is to say "Amin" (amen) after Surah al-Hamd. This rule, when applied to one praying individually is based on Ihtiyat (precaution), but if someone utters it believing that it has been ordained by Shariah (Islamic Law) it is haram (forbidden). There is no harm if someone utters it erroneously or under taqiyyah. (Islamic Laws by Ayatollah Sayed Sistani #1139)

Second, recite another complete Chapter of the Holy Qur'an (for example the short chapter *Surat al-Ikhlas*, number 112).

Bismillaahi'r-Rahmanir-Raheem	In the Name of God, the Merciful, the Compassionate
1. *Qul huwallaahu ahad*	1. Say: 'He is God, the One,'
2. *Allaahus samad*	2. God the Eternal and Besought of all,
3. *Lam yalid walam yulad*	3. Neither begetting nor begotten,
4. *Wa lam yakul lahu kufuwan ahad*	4. Nor is there anything comparable or equal to Him.

Ruku`: After completing the second chapter, the worshipper would say the *Takbir* (see above) and then bow down until the hands can be placed on the knees. The following *dhikr* (remembrance/glorification) is recommended to be recited audibly once in this position:

Subhaana rabbiy al-`adheemi wa bi hamdih
Glory be to my Lord, the Great, and praise belongs to Him
Or also ***Subhanallah*** (glory be to Allah) 3 times

Resume the standing position and recite audibly:

Sami`allaahu liman hamidah
God hears the one who praises Him

Say *Takbir*, then go into Prostration (*sujud*).

Sujud (plural for *sajdah*, meaning "prostration") is done by placing one's forehead on earth in a special manner, with the intention of humility before God.

 While performing the *sujud*, it is obligatory that both the hands (palms and thumbs at the minimum) and the knees, and both the big toes be placed on the ground. The following *dhikr* is recommended to be recited audibly in the *sujud* once:

Subhaana rabbiy al-a`laa wa bi hamdih
Glory be to my Exalted Lord, and praise belongs to Him
Or also ***Subhanallah*** (glory be to Allah) 3 times

The majority of scholars state that sajdah *should be performed on earth, and on those things that are neither edible nor worn, and on things which grow from earth (e.g. wood and leaves of trees). It is not permissible to perform* sajdah *on things that are used as food or dress (e.g. wheat, barley and cotton etc.), or on things that are not considered to be parts of the earth (e.g. gold, silver, etc.). And in the situation of helplessness, asphalt and tar will have preference over other non-allowable things.*[36]

After first *sajdah*, raise the forehead and sit up in a kneeling position (see illustration) with the ankle of the right foot in the sole of the left foot, with hands resting on the thighs and say *Takbir*, then recite audibly:

Astaghfirullaah rabbee wa atubu ilayh
I ask forgiveness of God, my Lord, and turn towards Him

---

[36] For example see *Islamic* Laws by Ayatollah Sayed Sistani #1085 and also *Islamic Laws* by Ayatollah Sayed Sadiq Shirazi Islamic pages 150-151

Repeat *Takbir* again. Repeat the *sajdah* again and then sit up in a kneeling position and say *Takbir*.

Sit up for a moment and then rise while saying audibly:

Bi hawlillaahi wa quwwatihi aqumu wa aq`ud
With God's help and through His power I stand and sit

Second *Rak`ah*
After regaining the upright posture, recite *Surat al-Fatiha* and another *Surah* of the Holy Qur'an as in the first *rak`ah*. Then say *Takbir*, and then do *Qunut*.

Qunut: In performing *Qunut*, it is *mustahab* (recommended) to raise the hands to the proximity/level of the face, aligning the palms of the hands side by side, fingers joined, with the exception of the thumbs, with the palms of the hands facing skywards, and one should look into the palms of the hands. It suffices to recite any *dhikr* one wishes, even if one said *Subhanallah* once.

Recite audibly the following or any other *du'a* (invocation) you choose:

Rabbanaa aatinaa fid-dunyaa hasanatan wa fil-akhirati hasanatan wa qinaa `adhaab an-naar

"O' our Lord! Bestow upon us good in this world and good in the Hereafter, and protect us from the torment of the fire" (Qur'an 2:201)

Ayatollah Sayed Sadiq Shirazi states it is mustahab *to perform* Qunut *in all prayers, obligatory and optional, and it should be performed before the* ruku' *of the second* rak`ah, *and as per* mustahab *precaution it should not be missed out in the obligatory* salat. *(Islamic Laws by Ayatollah Sadiq Sayed Shirazi page 156)*

Say *Takbir*, followed by the *ruku`*, then the two *sujud*, both as described for the first *rak`ah*

Tashahhud: After the second prostration resume the kneeling position, and recite audibly:

1. *Al-Hamdu lillah*
2. *Ash hadu an laa ilaaha illallaahu wahdahu laa shareeka lah,*
3. *wa ash hadu anna Muhammadan `abduhu wa rasuluh*
4. *Allaahumma salli `alaa Muhammadin wa Aale Muhammad*

1. All praise be to Allah
2. I bear witness that there is no god apart from Allah, Who is alone and without partners.
3. I also bear witness that Muhammad is His servant and His messenger.
4. O God, bless Muhammad and the progeny of Muhammad.

If you are performing the *Fajr* prayer, please skip the rest and go to section entitled **Completion.**

If you are performing the *Zuhr, Asr, Maghrib* or *`Isha* prayer, continue by standing up for the third unit while reciting *Bihawlillahi….* as described at the end of the section **First Rak`ah.**

Third *Rak`ah*

Tasbihat Arba`ah:* After regaining the upright posture, either recite silently *Surat al-Fatiha*, or recite silently *Tasbihat Arba`ah three times, as follows:

Subhaanallaahi wa'l hamdu lillaahi wa laa ilaaha illallaahu wallaahu akbar

Glory be to God, and praise be to God; there is no god but Allah, and Allah is the Greatest

Perform the *ruku`*, stand up momentarily and then do the two *sujud*. This is exactly as described under section **First Rak`ah**.

If you are performing the *Maghrib* prayers, recite the *Tashahhud* next. Then skip the rest and go to **Completion**.

If you are performing the *Zuhr*, `*Asr* or`*Isha* prayer, continue by standing up for the fourth *rak`ah* while reciting ***Bihawlillahi....*** as described at the end of the section **First Rak`ah**.

Fourth Rak`ah

This is identical to the third *rak`ah*. After the second prostration resume the kneeling position, and recite the *Tashahhud.*

Completion

After reciting the *Tashahhud* of the final *rak`ah*, recite the **Taslim** *(Salutation)* audibly, without deviating the face from the direction of the *Qibla*, which completes your prayer:

1. *As-salaamu `alayka ayyuhan nabiyu wa rahma tul laahi wa barakaatuh*

1. God's peace, mercy and blessings be upon you, O Prophet.

2. *As-salamu `alaynaa wa `alaa `ibaadillaa his saaliheen*

2. Peace be upon us, and upon the righteous servants of God.

3. *As-salamu `alaykum wa rahma tul laahi wa barakaatuh*

3. Peace be upon you [all], and God's mercy and blessings.

Thereafter proceed to say *Takbir* three times audibly. At this point, your prayer is completed.

Then, after the completion of your prayer, it is recommended to do sajdah shukr (prostration of thanks) and say Shukran lillah (Thank you, Allah!).

It is also recommended to do the Tasbihaat of Fatimah Zahra (as) which is:

1) "Allahu Akbar," recited 34 times
2) "Al-Hamdu lillah," recited 33 times
3) "Subhanallah," recited 33 times

Then you may proceed to do your own supplications in your own language or any of the recommended du'a that can be found in various books such as Mifatih ul Jinan by Sheikh Abbas Al-Qummi, Sahifa Sajjadiyya by Imam Sajjad (as), etc.

Why Say *Bismillah* Aloud?

It is narrated by Imam Hassan Al-Askari (as) that to recite the *Bismillah* <u>aloud</u> in <u>every</u> *salat* is a sign of a true believer.[37] It is also narrated that Imam Ali (as) used to say his *salat* in this way. We read from Dr. Muhammad al-Tijani al-Samawi:

> Such is the Holy Qur'an, and such is the Prophet whose conduct was the embodiment of the injunctions of the Holy Qur'an. *Ahl al-Sunnah wal Jama`a*, because of the intensity of their animosity towards Ali ibn Abu Talib and Ahl al-Bayt (peace be upon them), deliberately contradicted the latter in everything, so much so that their motto was to oppose Ali and his Shi`as in every aspect, even if that meant contradicting a *Sunnah* (tradition of the Prophet) which they themselves regard as authentic. Since Imam Ali was famous for reciting the *bismillah* audibly even while reciting the inaudible prayers in order to revive the Prophet's *Sunnah*, a number of the *sahaba* (companions) expressed their view that it is *makrooh* (disliked) to recite it in the prayers. So is the case with regard to holding the hands versus placing them on the sides, the supplication during the *qunoot*, in addition to other issues relevant to the daily prayers. [38] Anas ibn Malik, therefore, used to weep and complain thus: "By Allah! I hardly find anything being done anymore which the Messenger of Allah used to do." He was asked, "What about the prayers?" He said, "You have altered it, too."[39]

---

[37] *Karbala and Beyond* by Yasin T. al-Jibouri page 125

[38] *The Shi'a the Real Followers of the Sunnah* by Dr. Muhammad al-Tijani al-Samawi page 187 in the chapter The Sunnah and the Qur'an According to "Ahl al-Sunnah wal Jama`a"

[39] *Al-Bukhari, Sahih, Vol. 1*, p. 74

We follow the example of the Prophet and the Imams from his Ahl-ul-Bayt (as) who recited *bismillah* aloud. It was the *Umayyads* who were hostile to the family of the Prophet, who deviated from this practice to be different from the Shi'a.

Imam Nishaburi reports in his book *Tafsir Ghara'ib Al-Quran* that: "There is another charge that Ali (as) used to amplify in raising his voice in the *bismillah* and during the reign of the Umayyads they have exaggerated in preventing this practice in attempt to obliterate every trace for Ali (as)."

The first to start this practice was Mu'awiyah ibn Abu Sufyan.[40] So whoever says *salat* without reciting the *bismillah* aloud has contradicted the *sunnah* and followed the innovations of the Umayyad's in obliterating the traces of Ali (as), knowingly or unknowingly. This is why it is important to know the reasons behind the differences of opinion.

---

[40] Commentary of Surah Fatiha in the Holy Quran translated by S.V. Mir Ahmed Ali.

Takkatuf

(Folding the Hands in Salat)

While performing *salat* you will see that a lot of Muslims hold their hands in different positions while in *qiyam* (standing position). Some will fold their hands across their chest, some by their navel, and some let their hands hang by their sides. You probably asked yourself, "Why do they do these things?" Let us first look at the word *qiyam*. This word when looked up means: upright, erect. When you stand upright your arms should be straight as well. If your arms were folded then your body would be in *qiyam* but your arms would not be. To have the whole body erect would be the position of *qiyam*. According to *The Five Schools of Islamic Law* by Muhammad Jawad Al-Mughniyyah, all the 4 Sunni schools and the Shia school agree that holding the hands by the side is permissible. None of them states that *takkatuf* is obligatory.[41] The Shia scholars say that *takkatuf* will void your *salat*, because it is a later *bidah*.[42]

Placing the right hand over the left hand while standing in prayer is what is called *Takattuf.*

---

[41] The Five Schools of Islamic Law" by Muhammad Jawad Al-Mughniyyah page 91

[42] An unlawful and unauthorized addition into the religion

Al-'Allamah ibn al-Mutahhar al-Helli says in *Tathkirat al-Fuqahaa*: *al-Takkatuf* invalidates the prayer and it is placing the right over the left during recitation and the scholars of the Shia sect agree on this—al-Sheikh and al-Murtada both said—al-Baqir (as) said: "And do not make *Takkatuf* (placing right over left), for it is something that the Zoroastrians do."

Also Muhammad bin Muslim asked one of the Imams about the man who places in prayer his right hand over his left. He (as) replied: "That is (called) *al-Takkatuf*, do not do it."

Al-'Allamah Muhammad Hassan Najafi who was the head of the Shia sect in his time says in *Jawahir al-Kalam*:

"It was said about 'Umar that when they brought him the prisoners from the non-Arabs ('*Ajam*), they did *Takkatuf* (placing right over left) in front of him, so he asked about it and they told him that they did this as a sign of submission in front of their Kings, so he saw that it was good to do it for Allah in prayer but did not pay attention to the unpleasantness of imitating the Zoroastrians in *Shari'ah*."

al-'Allamah Najm-ul-Deen al-Tibsi says in *Al-Irsaal wal-Takkatuf bayn al-Sunnah wal-Bid'ah* pg.13-14:

"There are many narrations from Ahl ul-Bayt (as) prohibiting al-*Takkatuf* and describing it as being from Zoroastrianism"

And he also said on pg.18-19:

"It was said that it was innovated by the Caliph 'Umar bin al-Khattab, he took it from the non-Arab prisoners."

Ayatollah Sayed Sadiq al-Shirazi said in *Sharae'e al-Islam* by al-Helli, #235:

"It is what is called *'al-Takattuf'* and *al-Takkatuf* that the 'Aamah (Sunni's) practice, following the path of 'Umar bin al-Khattab, and 'Umar had taken it from the Zoroastrians then inserted it into *salat*, this was one of his innovations and it was never done by the Prophet (sawa) nor his Ah ul Bayt (as)."

Grand Ayatullah al-Khoei says in *Kitab al-Salat* vol. 4 pages 445-446:

"It is no secret that the act of *Takkatuf* was never practiced during the time of the great Prophet (sawa), even though it was narrated through several chains that do not come through us (Shia) thus they are all fabricated and false. Then we should not be hesitant to class it as one of the later innovations after his time. As for the time of the first caliph as it is said or most probably the second as we see in the narration, that when they brought the Persian prisoners to 'Umar, and he saw them in that state so he asked for the reason and they answered that this is what they do in front of their kings to glorify them, so he was pleased with it and ordered that it be done in prayer as Allah is more worthy of praise."

Why *Takbir* Three Times After *Salat*?

One of the characteristics of a believer is that after *taslim* in every obligatory prayer he must raise his hands up to his ears and then bring them back down to his thighs, repeating this action three times and each time say: Allahu Akbar. Ali ibn Ibrahim, Sayyid ibn Tauss, and Ibn Babwayh Qummi have reported that Imam Jafar Sadiq (as), through a very reliable chain of narration that Mufadhil ibn Amr asked the Imam about the justification of the three *takbirat* after *salat*. The Imam replied that the Holy Prophet (sawa) after the conquest of *Makkah* offered the *Zuhr* prayer along with his companions near the black stone. The Prophet (sawa) after *taslim* repeated the *takbir* three times and in each time doing so raised his hands and said the following *du'a*:

*"Laa ilaha illallahu wahdahu wahdah wahdah wanjaza wahdah
Wa nasara 'abdah wa 'izza jundah wa ghalabul ahzaha wahdah
Falahul mulku walahul hamd yuhyi wa yumitu wa huwa 'ala kulli shay in qadeer"*

I bear witness that there is no god but Allah, He is alone He is alone He is alone. And he fulfilled his promise and awarded victory to his slave, and dignified his soldiers, and dominated the parties by himself. So to him be the kingdom and to him be the praise. He gives life and death and he has power over everything.

Then the Prophet (sawa) turned his face towards his companions and emphasized not to abandon these three *takbirat* and *du'a* after every *salat*, and that whoever does so after *taslim*, he in fact thanks Allah for His bounties.

Also one of the main authorities of Sunni literature, *Sahih Muslim*, we see that Ibn Abbas narrates: "We knew that the Prophet had concluded his prayers when he recited the three *takbirat*."[43]

---

[43] *Sahih Muslim* 1:219, *Inquiries about Shia Islam*, page 68 by Sayed Moustafa Al-Qazwini

Hayya 'Ala Khayril 'Amal
(Hasten to the Best of Deeds)

This phrase was first introduced into the *adhan* by the Prophet (sawa) at *Ghadir Khumm*. *Ghadir Khumm* is a place outside of *Makkah* where the Prophet (sawa) told everybody to stop after returning from Hajj during the last year of his life. When they stopped, he called all the Muslims together and ordered Bilal (ra) to call the *adhan*. When Bilal reached "*hayya 'alal falah*" the Prophet (sawa) stopped him and said to repeat "*hayya 'ala khayril 'amal*" two times. This phrase means: Make haste towards the best of deeds.[44] The deed he was speaking of holds great importance and upon completing it the religion was perfected.[45] This deed was the appointment of Ali (as) as his successor.

After the Prophet's (sawa) martyrdom, Abu Bakr seized power while leaving the Prophet (sawa) unburied for three days, in spite of the Prophet's (sawa) appointment of Ali as the *khalif* (successor)! Abu Bakr and Umar conspired while the *Ahl-ul-Bayt* (as) were preparing the funeral rites. This is where the split came about in the community. Some sided with Ali (as) following the Prophet's (sawa) instructions. These people were (and are) called the Shia ("Shi'a" meaning follower, and the term here specifically referring to "followers of Ali"). Some sided with the usurper of *khalifat* Abu Bakr.[46] These followers of Abu Bakr and 'Umar are called the Sunni sect.

---

[44] Know Your Islam by Yousef Naljee

[45] Quran 5:3

[46] Those who didn't side with Abu Bakr found life very difficult. Please refer to my first book entitled *The Suffering of the Ahl ul Bayt and their Shia throughout History*

Bilal (ra) sided with Ali (as) and thus as a form of protest quit calling the *adhan* to show people how serious this was! Abu Bakr got very angry and upset with Bilal (ra) and exiled him to Syria. He later died and was buried there. He was replaced by someone else and that person was told not to recite the phrase *Hayya 'ala khayril 'amal.* The unjust rulers were afraid that if it were recited the people would remember the rightful claim of Ali (as) and realize the falsity of Abu Bakr's rule.[47]

As followers of the Prophet (sawa) we acknowledge Ali's (as) right and recognize him as the first Imam. Knowing this, we call the *adhan* with the phrase *Hayya 'ala khayril 'amal* as the Prophet (sawa) ordered it. This separates the followers of truth from the followers of falsehood.

---

[47] *Bilal of Africa* by Hussain Malika Ashtiyani

As-Salatu Khayrum min Nawm
(Prayer is Better than Sleep)

This phrase *As-Salatu khayrum min nawm* is said by the *ahl-us-sunnah* (Sunni sect) after *hayya 'alal falah* in the *adhan* of the morning prayer, but they do not say it in the *iqamah*.

In *The Five Schools of Islamic Law* p.129, it states that this phrase is NOT a *masnun* (traditional) part of the *adhan*, and this is the opinion of Shafi'i, who is one of the four leaders of Sunni Jurisprudence.

The cause for the disagreement is the question whether it was said or not during the lifetime of the Prophet (sawa) or whether it was during the time of 'Umar ibn Al-Khattab. Ishaq has said: "This thing has been innovated by the people" and Abu 'Isa said: "This phrase is something that the learned people have regarded with distaste. It is on the hearing which 'Abdullah ibn 'Umar left the mosque!"

It is reported that once when 'Umar was asleep he was awakened by a man named Malik using this phrase. 'Umar liked the phrase and incorporated it in the *adhan*. This is why, as mentioned above, some Sunni's disagree with this phrase. According to the scholars of the *Ahl-ul-bayt* this phrase is not to be said, as it is a *bidah*.[48]

---

[48] An unlawful and unauthorized addition into the religion

Why Prostrate on *Turbah*

Then I was guided author, Muhammad al-Tijani al-Samawi, writes:

"I asked about the piece of clay on which they put their foreheads during the prayers and they call it '*Al-Turbah al-Hussainiyyah.*' He answered, 'We all prostrate on the dust, but not for the dust, as some people claim that the Shia do, for the prostration is only for Allah, praise be to Him, the Highest. It is well established among our people, as well as among the Sunni's, that the most favorable prostration is on earth or on the non-edible produce of the earth, and it is incorrect to prostrate on anything else. The Messenger of Allah (sawa) used to sit on the dust, and he had a piece of clay mixed with straw, on which he used to prostrate. He also taught his Companions to prostrate on the earth or on stones, and forbade them from prostrating on the edges of their shirts. We consider these acts to be necessary and important.

Imam Zayn al-Abideen Ali ibn al-Hussain [may Allah bless them both] took a *Turbah* [a piece of clay] from near the grave of his father Aba Abdillah Hussain (as), because the dust there is blessed and pure, for the blood of the chief martyr was spilt on it. Thus, his followers continue with that practice up to the present day. We do not say that prostration is not allowed but on *Turbah*, rather, we say that prostration is correct if it is done on any blessed *Turbah* or stone, also it is correct if it is done on a mat which is made of palm leaves or similar material."[49]

---

[49] *Then I Was Guided*, by Dr. Muhammad al-Tijani al-Samawi in the chapter "A Meeting with Al Sayyid Muhammad Baqir al Sadr," page 44

The majority of *Shia* scholars state that *sajdah* should be performed on earth, and on those things that are neither edible nor worn, and on things which grow from earth (e.g. wood and leaves of trees). It is not permissible to perform *sajdah* on things that are used as food or dress (e.g. wheat, barley and cotton etc.), or on things that are not considered to be parts of the earth (e.g. gold, silver, etc.). And in the situation of helplessness, asphalt and tar will have preference over other non-allowable things.[50]

In the book *Inquiries about Shia Islam* page 68 by Sayed Moustafa Al-Qazwini we find the following:

"Other narrations say that the Holy Prophet (sawa) prohibited the Muslims from prostrating on materials other than the earth. One day he saw a man prostrating on some cloth from his turban. The Holy Prophet pointed to him and told him to remove his turban and to touch his actual forehead to the ground."[51]

Despite the immense heat of the ground, the Holy Prophet (sawa) and his companions used to prostrate on it. A great companion of the Holy Prophet, Jabbir ibn 'Abdullah al-Ansari says, "I used to pray the noon prayers with the Messenger of Allah and I used to take a bunch of pebbles in my palm to cool them because of the enormous heat so I could prostrate on them."[52]

Another companion of the Holy Prophet, Anas ibn Malik narrates, "We used to pray with the Messenger of Allah during the enormous heat, and one of us would take the pebbles in his

---

[50] For example see *Islamic Laws by Ayatollah Sayed Sistani #1085* and also *Islamic Laws by Ayatollah Sayed Sadiq Shirazi Islamic pages 150-151*

[51] al-Hiythami, *Sunan al-Bayhaqi*. Vol. 2. 105. Ibn Hajar, *al-Isabah li Ma'rifat al-Sahabah*. Vol. 2. 201.

[52] *Sahih al-Nisa'i*. Vol. 2. 204. al-Hiythami, *Sunan al-Bayhaqi*. Vol.1.

hand and, once they were cooled, put them down and prostrate on them."[53]

Al-Khabbab ibn al-Arth, another companion of the Holy Prophet says, "We complained to the Messenger of Allah about the intensity of the heat of the ground and its effects on our foreheads and palms (during prostration), and the Prophet did not excuse us from praying on the ground."[54]

During the times of the first, second, third, and fourth caliphs the Muslims used to prostrate on the dust. Abu Umayyah narrates that the first caliph, Abu Bakr used to prostrate and pray on the earth.[55]

Prostrating on the earth was also the habit of the *tabi'in* (those who did not see the Holy Prophet but met his companions). Masruq ibn al-Ajda', member of the *tabi'in*, a faithful jurist, and a student of 'Abdullah ibn Mas'ud made for himself a tablet from the dirt of *Madina* and used it to prostrate on, taking it with him on his trips, especially when he boarded ships.[56]

The people closest to the Holy Prophet (sawa), the *Ahl ul Bayt* (as), were also very firm in their practice of prostrating on the earth, and in doing so, were following the tradition of their grandfather, the Messenger of Allah. Imam Ja'far al-Sadiq (as), the sixth imam said, "Prostration is not permitted except on the earth and whatever grows from it except on those things that are

---

[53] al-Hiythami, *Sunan al-Bayhaqi.* Vol. 2. 105. *Nayl al-Awtar.* Vol. 2. 268.

[54] al-Hiythami, *Sunan al-Bayhaqi.* Vol. 2. 106.

[55] Al-Muttaqi al-Hindi, *Kanz al-Ummal.* al-Hiythami, *Sunan al-Bayhaqi. Sunan al-Kubra.* Vol. 4. 212. Vol. 2

[56] Ibn Sa'ad, *al-Tabaqat al-Kubra.* Vol. 6. 53.

eaten or made of cotton."[57]

When he was asked whether having one's turban touch the earth instead of the forehead was acceptable, he replied that this was not sufficient unless the forehead actually touched the earth. His companion and student, Hisham ibn al-Hakam asked him whether all seven positions (forehead, hands, knees, and big toes) needed to touch the earth during prostration. Imam al-Sadiq (as) replied that as long as the forehead touched the earth, there was no need for the other six areas to touch the earth as well.

Thus, people can use carpets or prayer rugs to pray on as long as the forehead itself touches the earth. However, prostrating by putting the forehead on a piece of cloth, carpet, nylon, sheet, wool, or anything that is not a product of the earth (excluding items which are eaten or worn; things which prostration is not permissible) would not be considered prostrating on the earth.

Besides the issue of validity of prostration, prostrating on the earth has very significant indications and lessons for the believer. Prostrating itself is a gesture of humility and insignificance before the Almighty, and if it is done on the dirt then it will have more effect than prostrating on a carpet. The Messenger of Allah says, "Make your faces dusty and cover your noses with dust."[58]

When Imam Ja'far al-Sadiq (as) was asked about the philosophy behind prostrating on the earth, he said, "Because prostration is surrendering and humility to the Almighty. Therefore, it shouldn't be on what is worn and eaten because people are slaves of what they eat and wear, and prostration is

---

[57] *Wasa'il al-Shi'ah.* Vol. 3. 592.

[58] *Al-Targhib wal-Tarhib.* Vol. 1. 581.

the worshipping of Allah, so one should not put his forehead during prostration on that which is worshipped by the people (food and clothing) and that which conceits people."[59]

The first to prostrate on the soil of *Karbala* (where Imam Husayn was beheaded and buried) was his son, Ali ibn al-Husayn Zayn al-Abidin (as) the fourth imam of the school of *Ahl ul Bayt*, the great-grandson of the Messenger of Allah. Immediately after he buried his father in Karbala, he took a handful of the soil, made the earth into a solid piece and used it to prostrate on.

After him, his son Imam Muhammad al-Baqir (as) and his grandson, Imam Ja'far al-Sadiq (as) did the same. Imam Zayn al-Abidin (as) and Imam al-Sadiq (as) made prayer beads from the burial dust of Imam Husayn (as), and Imam al-Sadiq (as) narrates that the daughter of the Messenger of Allah, Lady Fatima al-Zahra (as) used to carry prayer beads made from twisted wooden threads with which she would praise and glorify Allah, the Exalted. But after Hamzah ibn 'Abd al-Mutalib[60] was killed in the Battle of Uhud, she took the soil from his grave and made prayer beads from it and used them to glorify Allah. People learned her habit and did the same when Imam Husayn (as) was martyred; taking the soil of his grave and using it to make prayer beads.[61]"

In *Mifatihul Jinan* by Sheikh Abbas Al-Qummi we find the following about the merits of *Turbah*:

---

[59] *Wasa'il al-Shi'ah*. Vol. 3. 591.

[60] The uncle, close friend and beloved companion of the Prophet

[61] *Tarikh ibn Asakir*. Vol. 4. 342. Hafiz al-Kanji, *al-Kifayah*. 293.

Imam Rida (as) said "Whoever uses the rosary made of the clay of Imam Hussain's (as) tomb repeating the following statements with each bead Almighty Allah shall record for him six thousand excellent points, erase six thousand evil doings of him, raise him six thousand ranks and decide for him six thousand times of intercession.

- *Subhanallah* (Glory be to Allah)
- *Al-Hamdu lillah* (Praise be to Allah)
- *Laa ilaha illa allah* (There is no god but Allah)
- *Allahu Akbar* (God is the Greatest)"

Imam Sadiq (as) said "Whoever uses the rosary made of the clay of Imam Hussain's (as) tomb imploring for Almighty Allah's forgiveness one time only, shall be considered to have implored his forgiveness seventy times. Whoever holds in his hand such a rosary without uttering any statement of glorification, shall be considered to have uttered seven statements of glorification for each bead."

Reciting the name of Ali (as) in the *Adhan*

In the call to prayer you will notice the *Shia,* after bearing witness to the oneness of Allah and the prophethood of our beloved Prophet Muhammad (sawa) also bear witness to what is known as the third testimony (*shahadat-e thalitha*). This third testimony is bearing witness to the *wilayat* (guardianship) of the Commander of the Faithful, Imam Ali (as) by saying *"Ash-hadu anna Aliy-yan waliy-yullah."* Below are numerous sources below to show proofs of where this originates, that it is permissible to say, and also the opinions of the great *Shia* scholars about this matter.

Quran and Ahadith

Shaykh Abdullah Maraghi, a prominent Sunni scholar, in his book *As-Salafah fee Amrul Khilafah,* has mentioned the following two reports regarding the beginning of the third testimony:

1) Salman Farsi (ra) used to mention in adhan and iqamah, after the testimony of the messengership of the Messenger of Allah (sawa), the testimony to the mastership (wilayat) of Imam Amirul Momineen Ali (as). A companion came to meet the Holy Prophet (sawa) and asked: "O' Messenger of Allah, I heard a strange thing today, which I never heard before!" "What did you hear?" his eminence asked. He replied: "I saw Salman testify to the mastership (wilayat) of Ali ibn Abi Talib in the adhan after the testimony of prophethood! The Holy Prophet said: "You heard a nice thing."

2) A companion came to the Holy Prophet and asked: "O' Messenger of Allah, I saw Abu Zar say in the adhan, after the testimony of prophethood, he also testified to the mastership (wilayat) of Ali ibn Abi Talib! The Holy Prophet said: "You have forgotten what I said in Ghadir Khumm: Of whomsoever I am the master, Ali is also his master. One who breaks this pledge has not, but put himself in trouble."

On the basis of these two reports, the mention of I witness that Ali is the Wali of Allah in the adhan is having a long precedent and it originated during the lifetime of the Prophet (sawa) and he permitted it through silent approval.[62]

Shahadat-e-thalitha by Fatima Zahra (as) – The first words after her birth:

"Then Fatima (as) said: "I testify that there is no god but Allah, and My Father is Prophet of Allah (sawa) and Ali (as) is the leader of the custodians and my children are leaders of the tribes." [Ref: *Bihar Al Anwar* Vol.16 Pg.81]

Shahadat-e-thalitha in the *Dua* of Imam Sadiq (as):

"There is no god but you and you are our Lord. And Muhammad is your servant and your prophet and messenger. And Ali is the leader of the believers and the greatest proof and biggest sign and the greatest news in which people are confused."
[Ref: *Tehzibul Alkam* – Sheikh Tusi Vol.3 Pg.146]

---

[62] *Our Questions* by Ayatollah Hussain Tehrani page 499

Names of the Imams (as) on a Parchment written 2000 years before Adam (as):

Dawood bin Katheer ar-Riqqi has said:

I came to Abu Abdullah Jafar bin Muhammad as-Sadiq (as) in Medina and he said to me: "Why have you not visited us since so long, O Dawood?"

I said: "I had something to do in Kufa."

He (as) said: "Whom did you leave in Kufa?"

I said: "May my soul be sacrificed for you! I have left your uncle Zayd. I left him riding on a horse with his sword and calling loudly: "Ask me before you will miss me. I have great knowledge. I have known the abrogating and abrogated verdicts, the oft-repeated verses and the great Quran. Knowledge is between Allah and you."

He (as) said to me: "O Dawood, things have affected you."

Then He (as) called: "O Suma'a bin Mihran, bring me a basket of ripe dates!"

He brought him a basket of ripe dates. He took one, ate it, took the kernel out of his mouth and stuck it into the ground. It grew and fruited. He picked an unripe date from one of the bunches. He split it and took a piece of parchment out of it. He spread it, gave it to me and said to me: "Read it!"

It had two lines. The first line was "There is no god but Allah and Muhammad is the messenger of Allah." The second line was "Surely the number of months with Allah is twelve months since the day when He created the heavens and the earth, of these four being sacred, that is the right religion. Amir Al-Mumineen Ali bin Abu Talib, al-Hasan bin Ali, al-Husain bin Ali, Ali bin al-Husain, Muhammad bin Ali, Jafar bin Muhammad, Musa bin Jafar, Ali bin Musa, Muhammad bin Ali, Ali bin Muhammad, Hasan bin Ali, al-Khalaf al-Hujjah."

Then He (as) said: "O Dawood, do you know when this has been written in this piece of parchment?"

I said: "Allah, His Messenger and You are more aware!"

He (as) said: "Two thousand years before Allah had created Adam."
[Ref: *Al Gayba – Nu'mani* Chapter:4 Hadith:18 / *Taweel al-Aayat* Vol.1 Pg.203 / Bihar al Anwar Vol.24 Pg.243]

A Jew reciting *Shahadat-e-thalitha* while becoming a Muslim at the hands of Imam Ali (as):

Background: A Jew from the descendants of Prophet Dawood (as) came to Medina after the martyrdom of the Holy Prophet (sawa) and had a few questions. Imam Ali (as) answered his questions and hence he became a Muslim and said the following on the Hands of Imam Ali (as)…

The Jew said: "By Allah you are right. This has been mentioned in the book of my father Dawood (as). The book has been inherited by one after another until it has reached me." Then he took out the book written by Prophet Dawood (as) and said to Imam Ali (as): "Give me your hand! I witness that there is no god but Allah and Muhammad is the messenger of Allah. It is he, of whom the Prophet Moses (as) has informed. And I witness that you (as) are the jurisprudent of this *umma* and the guardian of the messenger of Allah."

Then Imam Ali (as) began to teach him the laws of Islam.

[Ref: *Al Gayba – Nu'mani* Chapter: 4 Hadith: 30 / *Bihar al Anwar* Vol.10 Pg.23]

"And those who stand firm in their testimonies (minimum 3 shahadat). And those who guard (the sacredness) of their worship. And such will be the honored ones in the Gardens (of Bliss)" [63]

The above verse of the Holy Quran clearly states in the Arabic text that the word testimonies is in the plural which means that we should stand firm on a minimum of 3 testimonies (*shahadah*) so as to enter heaven.

"Neither speak thy Prayer aloud, nor speak it in a low tone, but seek a middle course between."[64]

Jabir ibn Abdullah Ansari asks Imam Muhammad Baqir (as) regarding this verse of the Holy Quran. Imam Baqir (as) replied saying:

"Do not say the *Wilayat* of Imam Ali (as) in prayer aloud, but don't hide it from Ali (as). Recite it in a middle tone until I give you the permission to recite/declare it openly. This permission was granted on the day of *Ghadeer-e-Khum*."

[Ref: *Tafseere Noor-uth-Thaqlain* Vol. 3 Pg. 235, *Tafseer-e - Ayyashi, Tafseer-e-Saafi, Tafseer-e-Burhaan*]

"The nature made by Allah in which he has made men."[65]

---

[63] *Quran* 70:33-35

[64] *Quran* 17:110

[65] *Quran* 30:30

Imam Muhammad Baqir (as) says regarding the above verse of the Holy Quran:

"That nature (Fitra) is 'There is no God but Allah, Muhammad is the Prophet of Allah, Ali Amir-al-Momineen is the Wali of Allah'.

[Ref: *Tafseer-e-Burhaan* Vol:3 Pg:262 and *Tafseer-e-Furaat*]

Imam Jafar As Sadiq (as) when asked about the verse of the Quran "And an announcement from Allah and His Messenger, to the people (assembled) on the day of the Great Pilgrimage" [9:3] said: ... Allah named him (Ali) *Adhan* from Allah. This (Adhan) is the name that Allah descended from the heaven for Ali (as).

[Ref: *Taweel-ul-Ayat* Pg.204 and *Bihar Al Anwar* Vol.35 Pg.293 and *Ma'ni Al Akhbar* Pg.298]

Views of Shia Scholars:

1) *Faqih-e-Ahl ul Bayt* (as) Muhammad Baqir Waheed Bahbani Hairi:
Whatever I have said proves the presence of *Shahadat* of Ali-un-*Wali-Allah*. Because it's being found in the general Hadith suffices and above this no other Hadith is required. Because it's said that when you do Muhammad's (saww) *dhikr*, do Ali's (as) *dhikr* as well. Hence there is no harm that we include this in *Adhan* and *Iqamat* as a *Juz* (part).

[Ref: *Al-Hidaya Fi Juziyat-ul-Shahadat-e-Wilayat*, Pg: 14]

2) *Faqih-e-Ahl ul Bayt* (as) Abul Qasim Khoei:

We don't need any Hadith to prove "Ali-un-Wali-Allah" in the *Adhan* and *Iqamat*, because *Wilayat* is a means for Completion of *Risalat* and strengthening of *Iman*. And *Wilayat* is 1 of those 5 things that are the basis of *Deen*. It is a clear sign and means of identification of Shia.
[Ref: *Mustanad Urwat-ul-Wusqa*, Vol:2, Pg:288
3) *Faqih-e-Ahl ul Bayt* (as) Abd-un-Nabi Iraqi:

There are more than 10 Authentic Hadith regarding *shahadat-e-Thalitha*. My opinion is that *Shahadat-e- Thalitha* is part of *Adhan* and *Iqamat*. The one who says that Ali-un-Wali-Allah is not proven in *Adhan* and hence is *Bid'at* and *Haraam*, then this is a misunderstanding of a person who does not have knowledge of *Fiqh*.
[Ref: *Al-Hidaya Fi Kaun-un-Shahadat Bil-Wilayah Fil-Adhan and Wal Iqamah Juzi Kasair-ul-Ajzia*, Pg:37 and *Al Hidaya Fi Juziyat-ul-wilayah*, Pg:161]

4) *Faqih-e-Ahl ul Bayt* (as) Mirza Aaqa Istehbaani:

Shahadat-e-Thalitha is a *Juz* (part) in *Adhan* and *Iqamat*.
[Ref: *Sharh Risalat-ul-Huqooq*, Vol: 3, Pg:113]

5) *Faqih-e-Ahl ul Bayt* (as) Sayed Muhammad Shirazi

Ash-hadu anna Ali-an-Wali-Allah is a *Juz* (Part) of *Adhan*.
[Ref: *Al Fiqh*, Vol: 9, Chapter on *Adhan*]

6) *Faqih-e-Ahl ul Bayt* (as) Muhammad Taqi Mamqani:
The *Shahadat-e-Wilayat* is proven for most of the Historians. Authentic are there on *Shahadat-e-Thalitha*. Hence taking it to be *Juz* (part) will not be wrong.
[Ref: *Sahifat-ul-Abraar*, Vol: 2, Pg: 186]

7) *Faqih-e-Ahl ul Bayt* (as) Abdur Razzak Muqarram:

Examining the numerous traditions that prove that the Holy Prophet many times clarified that the *Wilayat* of his Successor is the completion of the 2 testimonies (*Shahadatain*), confirms that in the very life of the Prophet *Shahadat-e-Thalitha* after the *Shahadatain* was in the *Adhan* etc. Although it was difficult for Prophet Muhammad (sawa) to make the open declaration of *Wilayat* of Ali (as) as obligatory because there were many people who would not accept the Merits of Ali (as) [out of prejudice]. And how could they be satisfied with such an order that was a step in taking away the Successor ship from other than Imam Ali (as)?

[Ref: *Sirr-ul-Eeman*, Pg: 14]

8) *Faqih-e-Ahl ul Bayt* (as) Ali Madad Qaini:After knowing the narration of Imam (as) "Whoever say's La ilaha Illallah Muhammadur Rasool-ul-lah, he should say Ali-un Ameer ul Mumineen Wali-Ullah." It is not difficult to believe that the Imam (as) was indicating that *Shahadat-e-Thalitha* is a *Juz* (part) of *Adhan*.
[Ref: *Sirr-ul-Eeman*, Pg: 56]

9) *Faqih-e-Ahl ul Bayt* (as) Ibrahim Istehbati Shirazi Najafi:

Shahadat-e-Thalitha is a *Juz* (part) of *Adhan*.
[Ref: *Risalate Amaliya Zakhiratul Ibaad*, Pg: 46]

10) *Faqih-e-Ahl ul Bayt* (as) Sayed Husain Tabrizi:

In some narrations there exits the declarations of *Wilayat* like Sheikh Sadooq has quoted. It becomes evident from the words of Sheikh Sadooq and Sheikh Toosi that it has come in authentic narrations that *Wilayat* and *Risalat* are into one another and that the names of Prophet (saww) and Amir-ul-Mumineen (as) are always taken together.

[Ref: *Qawaid-ud-Deen* Pg: 227]

11) *Faqih-e-Ahl ul Bayt* (as) Muhammad Taqi Majlisi

It's possible that this (*Shahadat-e-Thalitha*) would be a *Juz* (part) if there had been no *Taqiyya*.
[Ref: *Rauzat-ul-Muttaqeen*, Vol: 2, Pg: 246]

12) *Faqih-e-Ahl ul Bayt* (as) Sheikh Muhammad Raza Najafi:

Shahadat-e-Thalitha not being a *Juz* (part) of *Adhan* is due to *Taqiyya*.

[Ref: *Sirr-ul-Eeman*, Pg: 41]

13) *Faqih-e-Ahl ul Bayt* (as) Sayed Sadiq Shirazi:

"Evidently the phrase 'Ash-hadu anna Aliy-yan waliy-yullah' is the integral part of both *adhan* and *iqamah*, as some narrations point to that."

[Ref: *Islamic Laws* by Ayatollah Sayed Sadiq Shirazi page 135]

Saying Ali's name in *tashahhud* is a recommended (*mustahab*) act

Someone asked Imam Muhammad Baqir (as) as to what is to be recited in the *qunoot* and *Tashahhud* of Prayer.

Imam Replied saying: "Recite that seems best, if this would have been fixed (as to what is to be recited) then people would have been perished."

[Ref: *Furu-e-Kaafi* Vol: 3 Pg: 337 and *Khulasat-al-Haqaiq* vol: 1 pg: 255]

Some one asked Imam Muhammad Baqir (as) as to what is the minimum *dhikr* to be recited in the *Tashahhud* of Prayer.

Imam (as) replied saying: "Recite *Shahadatain*" (i.e. 2 *shahadat*).
[Ref: *Furu-e-Kaafi Vol*: 3 Pg: 337]

Sheikh Sadooq also accepts this and he says the following in his *Amaali*: "Sufficient for *Tashahhud* is the 2 testimonies and any more than that is worship (*ibadat*)."

[Ref: *Amaali* – Sheikh Sadooq]

Tashahhud of Imam Jafar As Sadiq (as):

"...... I bear witness that no god but Allah alone with no partner and I bear witness that Muhammad is His slave and His Messenger.....I bear witness that you are the best Lord and that Muhammad is the best Messenger and that Ali is the Best *Wasi* and Imam....."[66]

[Ref: *Fiqh-e-Majlisi* Pg: 29]

Faqih-e-Ahl ul Bayt (as) Sayed Ahmad Mustanabad says the following in his book *Al Qatra*

"I finish this chapter with that *Tashahhud* which Imam Jafar Sadiq (as) used to recite in Prayer because have heard from a few people that they are in denial of the Third *Shahadah* in *Adhan*

---

[66] Ashhadu an laa ilaha illal lah, wa ashhadu anna muhammadan abduhu wa rasuluh, wa anna 'aliyan ni'mah wali, allahumma sali 'ala muhammadin wa aale muhammad is how this should be said if added as a mustahab act in tashahhud according to the view of Ayatollah Sayed Sadiq Shirazi

and *Iqamat*, although Sheikh Tabrisi in his book *Ehtejaaj* has quoted the following hadith from Imam Jafar Sadiq (as)":

Imam Jafar Sadiq (as) says: "When any one from you says 'La ilaha illa Allah, Muhammadan Rasool Allah' then he must say Alian Wali Allah."

[Ref: *Al-Ehtejaaj* Vol: 1 Pg: 230 / *Bihar Al Anwar* Vol: 27 Hadith: 1]

Sayed Ahmad Mustanabat continues by saying:

"This means that with the declaration of *Tauheed* and *Risalat*, the declaration of *Wilayat* of Imam Ali (as) should also be necessarily given. People are ignorant of the fact that based on the above hadith of Imam Jafar Sadiq (as) the declaration of the *Wilayat* of Imam Ali (as) is among the recommended acts (*mustahabat*) of Prayer."

"Below I quote the *Tashahhud* of Imam Jafar Sadiq (as) because its meaning is very in depth and high and it's very advantageous for those who think and ponder over it. This is quoted in the book *Fiqh-e-Majlisi* by Muhammad Taqi Majlisi and is as follows:

> ...... I bear witness that no god but Allah alone with no partner and I bear witness that Muhammad is His slave and His Messenger.....I bear witness that you are the best Lord and that Muhammad is the best Messenger and that Ali is the Best Wasi and Imam.....

[Ref: *Al-Qatra* Vol: 1 Pg: 328, (URDU – *al Qatra* vol: 2 pg 92/93)]

Faqih-e-Ahl ul Bayt (as) Sheikh Abdul Haleem:

Sheikh Abdul Haleem quoting the narration of *Tashahhud* with the Third *Shahadah* states:

"Some people consider the tradition of *Tashahhud* which is different from the one which is known among worshippers, as strange and shocking. And the truth is that there is no valid reason to be surprised in this because of the following reasons:

a) The way of *Tashahhud* which is common in our obligatory and recommended prayers is because that has become well known and famous among us and we recite it repeatedly and the same form of *Tashahhud* is present is the *Taudhihul Masail* (book of laws) of our Scholars and the forms of *Tashahhud* is not quoted in the *Taudhihul Masail* although in our books of *Hadith* and *Fiqh* there are many different forms of *Tashahhud* narrated from the Imams (as).

b) *Faqih* Sheikh Muhammad Husain Najafi in his book *Jawahir-al-Kalam* while discussing about *Tashahhud* says, "The worshipper has the right to recite *Tashahhud* based on any narration and it's not in any way proven that a specific form of *Tashahhud* is obligatory. In fact the lengthy *Tashahhud* based on the narration from Abu Baseer can also be recited. Hence any narration of *Tashahhud* from the Imam's (as) can be recited in Prayer."

c)   All that is said by Sheikh Yusuf Behrani in his book *Hadaiq-un-Nazira* can be summarized as, "It is well known among the people that the *Tashahhud* with *Shahadatain* (2 declarations) is obligatory while the *Tashahhud* with more than 2 declarations is considered recommended."

d) It is quoted in *Al-Kaafi* that someone asked Imam Muhammad Baqir (as) as to what is to be recited in the *qunoot* and *Tashahhud* of Prayer.

Imam Replied saying: "Recite that seems best, if this would have been fixed (as to what is to be recited) then people would have been perished."

This narration is also present in *Tehtheeb* and *Wasail-ush-Shia*.

The various narrations of *Tashahhud* which are found in our books of narrations such as in *Man La Yah Dharul Faqih* and *Mustadrakul Wasail*, the count of these narrations goes well above 12. Hence it is quite normal to be surprised about this narration of *Tashahhud*.

The lengthy *Tashahhud* narrated from Abu Baseer which is quoted in the books *Tehtheeb and Wasail* is considered as the most superior *Tashahhud* by Sheikh Muhammad Husain Najafi. And the next most superior *Tashahhud* is the one quoted by the Lover of Ahl ul bayt (as), author of the book *Hadaiq-un-Nadhira* which is quite similar to the *Tashahhud* quoted by *Faqih* Sayed Ahmad Mustanabat in his book *Al-Qatra*, this *Tashahhud* also contains the words "I bear witness that Ali is the Best *Wali*." This narration of *Tashahhud* is also quoted by Sheikh Noori in his book *Mustadrakul Wasail*. This *Tashahhud* is narrated by our Imams (as) and our *Fuqaha* and Scholars.

Hence don't get swept away by the talk of those who oppose these narrations of *Tashahhud*. Many have been swept in this wave of confusion. Beware of them. Beware of them. Beware of them. And seek the intercession of Imam Az-Zaman (atfs) that he may keep us safe from every conflict.

[Ref: *Shahadat-e-Salisa Al-Muqaddasa* Pg: 224-230]

Faqih Husain Baksh Jadah in his *Taudhihul Masail* (book of laws) 'Anwar-ush-Shariya dar Fikh-e-Jafariya' quotes the following *Tashahhud* from Imam Rida (as):

"… I bear witness that no god but Allah alone with no partner and I bear witness that Muhammad is His slave and His Messenger… I bear witness that you are the best Lord and that Muhammad is the best Messenger and that Ali is the Best Wali… O Allah sends Blessings on Muhammad Al Mustafa and Ali Morteza and Fatima Az Zehra and Hassan and Hussain, and the Imam's from the progeny of Taha and Yaseen."

[Ref: *Anwar-ush-Shariya dar Fiqh-e-Jafariya* Pg: 58]

Sayed Muhammad Husaini Baghdadi was asked a question on the permissibility of recital of *Tashahhud* of Imam Jafar as Sadiq quoted in the book *Al-Qatra* by *Faqih-e-Ahl ul Bayt* (as) Sayed Ahmad Mustanabat (which in turn quotes from *Fiqh-e-Majlisi*), also taking support from the following hadith of Imam Sadiq (as) quoted in *Ehtejaaj-e-Tabrisi*:

Imam Jafar Sadiq (as) says: "When any one from you says 'La ilaha illa Allah, Muhammadan Rasool Allah' then he must say Alian Wali Allah.' "

[Ref: *Al-Ehtejaaj* Vol: 1 Pg: 230 / *Bihar Al Anwar* Vol: 27 Hadith: 1]

Sayed Muhammad Husaini Baghdadi in reply said that "These are *mo'tabar* (respectable) narrations and acting on these is permitted."[67]

---

[67] Please refer to the web page "Shahadat-e-Salisa" for all of the links and scanned pages of the fatwa's and books referenced. www.shahadat-e-salisa.com

Salam* on the *Imam's (as)* after *Tashahhud:

Peace be upon you O Prophet and his blessings and grace be upon you! Peace be upon you all messengers and angels and prophets. Peace be upon the Guided Imams who guide. Allah's peace be on us and upon all pious servants of Allah.

[Ref: *Mustadrak Al Wasail* Vol.5 Pg.9 and *Bihar Al Anwar* Vol.82 Pg.287 and *Al Balad-ul-Ameen* Pg.8]

Why the Hatred?

Who is this man and why do they hate him so much? What did he do to make them curse him from the pulpits for over 80 years? Why did they disassociate from him and punish the ones who loved him by death? Some they tortured by cutting out their tongues, others they killed, crucifying them, cutting off their heads and even burying some alive!

What did this man do to them for them to confiscate his wife's property and source of income, leaving him and his family in the clutches of poverty? Why did they hate him so much that they waged civil wars against him? What drove them to set fire to his house, kicking the door in and smashing his beloved wife in-between, thus killing their unborn child?

Why did they hate him so much that they dragged him by the point of the sword to force his allegiance to the self-appointed ruler of the time? What did this man do to produce such hatred that they killed him while he was in prostration to his Lord?

Was this not the only man ever born inside the Holy Kabah? Was not this man raised by the Apostle of Allah (sawa) since he was five years old, following his every footstep? Was he not the first man to accept the message of Al-Islam? Was he not the first to offer salat with the Messenger of Allah? Was he not the only one, besides Prophet Muhammad (sawa), who never bowed down before an idol?

Was not this the same man who slept in the bed of the Prophet (sawa) readily risking his own life for the safety of Allah's Messenger (Quran, 2:207)? Was not this the greatest warrior in Al-Islam? Did not his steadfastness in battle earn him the title "Lion of Allah"? Was it not him who was the only one from amongst the Muslims to stand up against the pagan warrior, Amr, at the Battle of the Trench? Was it not him who cut this disbeliever in two saving the *deen* of Al-Islam? Was not this man the one who conquered the Jewish fort of *Khaybar* after others failed in their attempts?

Was not this man the same one Allah commands us to love in the *Holy Quran* (42:23), and purified him from all sins (*Quran* 33:33), and made it binding on us to obey him (*Quran* 5:55 and 4:59)?

Was it not this man who married the leader of the women of paradise, who gave birth to his two sons, the leaders of the youths of paradise? Was this not the same person the Apostle (sawa) appointed as his successor on numerous occasions? Was this not the same man upon whom being appointed the successor, Allah perfected the religion (*Quran* 5:3)?

Was this not the same person Allah defines as the "self" of the Prophet (sawa), being that they were created from the same light (Quran 3:61)?

Was he not the one who, instead of rushing off for political power, stayed with the body of the Prophet (sawa) and performed his burial rights?

If all this is true, how can these people still hate this man and frown at the mention of his name? Did not the Prophet (sawa) say that without offering blessings on this man the *salat* will not be accepted? Was this man any other than the cousin and son-in-law of the Prophet (sawa), Ali ibn Abu Talib (as)?

Some Important Hadith to Remember Regarding the Ahl-ul-Bayt (as)

1. Imam Ali (as) said: "People often hate those things that they don't understand." (*Nahjul Balagha* #172)

2. Imam Ali (as) said: "Whoever loves us, members of the Prophet's family, should be prepared to face destitution." (*Nahjul Balagha* #111)

3. Imam Sadiq (as) said: "It is surprising to hear people claim that they have derived all their knowledge from the Prophet (sawa) and having acted accordingly they are guided. And they believe that we, Ahl-ul-Bayt, have not derived his knowledge, nor have we been guided by him, in spite of being his family members and descendants! The revelation descended in our homes and from us the knowledge reached the people. Do you believe that they knew and were guided while we remained ignorant and lost? This is indeed impossible!" (*Al-Amaali* by Shaykh Saduq)

4. The Prophet (sawa) said: "What has happened to some people in my *ummah* who become cheerful and jubilant when Ibrahim (as) and the progeny of Ibrahim are mentioned to them, but when I and my progeny are mentioned they detest it and frown at it?! By He who sent me as a truthful prophet, if a person dies after having performed the deeds of 70 prophets but he has no liking for the authority of our Ahl-ul-Bayt, Allah will not accept any of his obligatory or voluntary acts of worship!" (*Al-Amaali* by Shaykh Saduq)

5. Narrated by Ibn Abbas that the Prophet (sawa) said: "Cling steadfastly to the affection for us, the Ahl-ul-Bayt. For whoever meets Allah with our love in his heart shall enter paradise by our intercession. By He who controls Muhammad's (sawa) breath, the acts and deeds of a servant shall not benefit him except coupled with our recognition and love!" (*Al-Amaali* by Shaykh Saduq)

6. Imam Ali (as) said: "Whoever loves us, his faith will benefit him and his works will bring him close to Allah. Whoever does not love us, his faith will not benefit him and his works will not bring him close to Allah even though he should strive night and day in prayer and fasting." (*Kitab Al-Irshad* by Sheikh Mufid)

7. Imam Sadiq (as) said: "We are those that obedience to whom Allah has made an obligation. Nothing is proper for the people except to know us, nor are the people absolved from being ignorant about us. He who knows us is a believer (*mu'min*) and he who knows us and denies us is a disbeliever (*kafir*). He who neither knows us nor denies us is misguided, until he returns to the path of guidance, which Allah has made an obligation for him as a binding obedience to us. If he dies in his misguidance then Allah will do with him what he pleases."
(*Usul Al-Kafi* vol. 1 Al-Usul pt. 2-4 "The Book of Divine Proof," pg.60)

8. Imam Baqir (as) said: "The one who is unaware of the oppressions done upon us, the one who is oblivious of the snatching away of our rights, and the one who is not aware of the misbehavior of the *ummah* towards us, surely he is among those oppressors."
(*Bihar ul-Anwar,* vol. 55, p. 77; *Eqaabul Aamaal*, p.208)

9. Abu Zar (ra) narrated that the prophet (sawa) said to Ali (as): "O' Ali, Allah has made me and you from the same tree. I am its root and you are its branch. Allah will throw a man into hell by his face if he cuts its branch!" (*Abu Zar, The Great Companion of the Prophet*)

10. The Prophet (sawa) said: "The example of my household is that of Noah's (as) ship. Whoever boards it will get rescued and the one who opposes the boarding of it will drown." (*Discourses of the 14 Infallibles*)

11. Imam Baqir (as) said: "If a man keeps standing the whole night for *salat*, keeps on fasting during the day, gives out all his wealth as alms, and performs *hajj* all the years of his life while he does not recognize the guardianship of the vicegerent of Allah so as to love him and perform all his practices under his guidance and leadership does not have any right out of his rewards and is not from among the faithful." (*Discourses of the 14 Infallibles*)

12. Imam Baqir (as) said: "The person who serves Allah according to a religion so putting himself in great inconvenience and hardship for it, and doesn't have an Imam fixed by Allah, then his endeavor is unaccepted and he is lost, gone astray, and a wandering person in a state of perplexity. Allah is the enemy to his practices and his example is that of a sheep that has lost her shepherd and herd wandering here and there all day long. And by Allah, similarly, in this *ummah* too anybody who starts a morning in a condition that he doesn't believe in the Imam appointed by Allah, an Imam who is apparent, evident, just, and equitable. He will start the morning in a condition that he is gone astray and perplexed. And if he dies in this very condition he will die a death of disbelief (*Kufr*) and hypocrisy (*Nifaq*)." (*Discourses of the 14 Infallibles*)

---

13. Imam 'Askari (as) said: "An age will approach when people's faces would be laughing and their hearts would be dark, bleak, and dirty. The *sunnah* to them would be *bidah* and *bidah* would be considered *sunnah* among them. The faithful would be belittled and debased among them and the transgressors would be honorable and respected among them. Their lords and chiefs would be ignorant and aggressive ones. And the religious scholars would be on the threshold of aggressors and tyrants." (*Discourses of the 14 Infallibles*)

14. The Prophet (sawa) said "Allah said: 'I will punish every group of Muslims who recognized the leadership of any unjust ruler whom I did not select, even if the individuals of such a group are pious and fear Allah. Likewise, I will forgive every group of Muslims who recognized exclusively the leadership of the just imams (as) whom I appointed, even if the individuals of such a group wrong themselves and commit bad deeds." (*Fadail al Shiah* - Hadith #12)

15. Ibn Abbas asked the Holy Prophet (sawa) to advise him. The Prophet (sawa) said "I advise you to love Ali ibn Abu Talib (as). I swear by Allah who sent me as a Prophet that Allah will not accept the good deeds of any slave without first questioning him about his love for Ali (as), and Allah knows the truth. So if the slave had the *wilayat* (guardianship), Allah will accept all the deeds of the slave, despite his shortcomings. If the slave did not have the *wilayat*, Allah will not question him about anything else and will order him to be taken to Hell." *(Bisharat al-Mustafa,* pg. 64, Hadith 9; *Amal al-Tusi,* vol. 1, pg. 104; *Bihar al-Anwar,* vol. 16, pg. 370 and vol. 28, pg. 157, *Tawil al-Ayaat,* vol. 1, pg. 277)

16. Imam Ali (as) said said "If a man worships Allah between *rukn* and *maqam* and fasts every single day of his entire existence without believing in our *wilayat*, he will not benefit in any way."
    (*Bisharat al-Mustafa*, pg. 402, Hadith 30)

17. The Prophet (sawa) said "The dwellers of paradise are those who obey me and submit to Ali ibn Abi Talib (as) after me and accept his *wilayat* (guardianship). The inmates of the fire are those who deny his *wilayat*, breach the covenant and fight against Ali (as) after me."
    (*Bisharat al-Mustafa*, pg. 212, hadith 2; *Bihar a-Anwar*, vol 39, pg 208)

18. Imam Sajjad (as) "Allah has made 5 religious duties mandatory and everything Allah makes mandatory is beautiful; *Salat, zakat, hajj*, fasting, and our *wilayat* (guardianship). People obeyed Allah in the first 4 and ignored the 5th. I swear by Allah that the first 4 are not complete without the 5th."
    (*Bisharat al- Mustafa*, pg 160, hadith 143; *Bihar al-Anwar*, vol 23, pg 105)

19. The Prophet (sawa) said "If everyone loved Ali ibn Abi Talib, Allah would not have created hell."
    (*Bisharat Al-Mustafa*, pg 114; *Bihar Al-Anwar*, vol 39, pg 249; *Amali* As-Saduq, pg 523; *Kashf Al-Ghummah*, vol 1, pg 99; *Manaqib Al-Khawarezmi*, pg 28; *Tawil Al-Ayat* ,vol 2, pg 497)

20. Ibn Abbas asked the Prophet (sawa) "Is there anyone who hates Ali (as)?" The Prophet (sawa) replied "Yes, some people who think they are from my nation hate him and they have nothing to do with Islam. One of the signs of those who hate Ali (as) is that they elevate people who are lower than Ali (as) above Ali (as)."
(*Bisharat al Mustafa* ,pg 64, hadith 9; *Amal* at Tusi, vol 1, pg 104; *Bihar al Anwar,* vol 16, pg 370 and vol 28, pg 157; *Tawail al Ayaat* ,vol 1, pg 277)

"Praise be to Allah Who made perfect His religion and completed His favor with the establishment of the commander of the faithful, Ali ibn Abu Talib's (as) love and authority! Praise be to Allah Who blessed us to be among those who cling and hold to the love and authority of the commander of the faithful and all the Imams, peace be upon them all!"

DUA FARAJ

O' GOD, BLESS MUHAMMAD AND THE FAMILY OF MUHAMMAD.

O' GOD, BE FOR YOUR REPRESENTATIVE, THE HUJJAT (PROOF), SON OF AL-HASAN, YOUR BLESSINGS BE ON HIM AND HIS FOREFATHERS, IN THIS HOUR AND IN EVERY HOUR, A GUARDIAN, A PROTECTOR, A LEADER, A HELPER, A PROOF, AND AN EYE UNTIL YOU MAKE HIM LIVE ON THE EARTH, IN OBEDIENCE (TO YOU), AND CAUSE HIM TO LIVE IN IT FOR A LONG TIME.

O' GOD, BLESS MUHAMMAD AND THE FAMILY OF MUHAMMAD.

Other Books from Mateen J. Charbonneau

Study and see how the Family of the Prophet (as) was treated after the martyrdom of our beloved Prophet (sawa). How the Prophet (sawa) was poisoned, how his beloved daughter Fatima (as) was crushed behind the door, whipped and made to miscarriage her unborn son Muhsin (as) all while they were setting fire to her house while her children, the masters of the youths of paradise Hassan (as) and Hussain (as), were inside. How they stole her land of Fadak and source of income as a way to put economic sanctions on them. How Imam Ali (as) was made to suffer under the rule of these oppressive rulers who stole his rights. How he was killed him by a fatal blow of a sword while he was in prostration to his Lord. How they tortured and killed his followers, the Shia, by cutting out their tongues, burying them alive inside of walls, crucifying them, exiling them, cutting off their heads and the list goes on. How they poisoned Imam Hassan (as) then obstructed his body from being buried beside his Grandfather the Messenger of Allah (sawa). How they brutally massacred Imam Hussain (as), his family, friends and even his 6 month old baby, none of whom had food or water for three consecutive days. How they imprisoned his women and children and made them march from Karbala to the prison of Damascus while whipping them and with all of the heads of their loved ones mounted on spears in the front of the army of these devils. How all of the Imams to follow, except Imam Mahdi (atf), were all killed by poison.

Find in-depth narrations of these stories and more in the book, *The Suffering of the Ahl ul Bayt (as) and Their Followers (Shia) Throughout History*, **by Mateen J. Charbonneau, available at Amazon.**

www.mateenjc.com

In researching Islamic history I have found in many cases that during the life time of the Holy Prophet (*sawa*), and also during the times of the twelve righteous Imams from his Holy Household (Ahl-ul-Bayt), some of the Christians stood up for the members of Holy Household when they were oppressed. It makes one wonder, why did these Christians support and defend the Prophet (*sawa*) and his pure family, when they belonged to a different religion? The Prophet and his family's characters were so noble that even the idol worshippers at the time of the holy Prophet (*sawa*), who hated him, could not come up with anything bad to say about his morals. The Prophet's title, even before proclaiming his Prophethood, was *"The Trustworthy"* (*Al-Ameen*) and *"The Truthful"* (*As-Saadiq*). These Holy personalities shined their light on everyone they came in contact with. It was amazing for people to witness such sublime morality in a human being, as they treated everyone with fairness and justice.

The Christians felt safe under the true Islamic government during Prophet's (*sawa*) and Imam Ali's (as) rule, and all of their rights were protected under their rulership.

The Prophet (*sawa*) and his pure family (as) felt that it was their duty to help their fellow human being in need. When the Christians witnessed the Prophet's (*sawa*) family being oppressed, some of the Christian monks acknowledged the right of their divine leadership (Imamate) and they stood up for justice and died defending them.

In this humble attempt I have compiled some historical accounts from the life of Prophet Muhammad (*sawa*) and his Family's treatment towards Christians during their respected times. Also, I have included historical accounts of Christians who protected the Holy Prophet (*sawa*) and some who gladly laid down their lives for his Holy Family (*as*). I hope this book will show the reader about how the Prophet (sawa) and his family demonstrated the true relationship between Islam and Christianity and how it should be today.

This is the Islam that was practiced by Prophet Muhammad (*sawa*) and his Family, not the Islam which was hijacked, and is still hijacked, by the corrupt rulers after the Prophet's (*sawa*) martyrdom.

Prophet Muhammad (*sawa*) treated everyone with justice and equality, but the rulers who took away the divine leadership from his family, excessively performed terrible deeds in the name of Islam. We need to recognize the distorted actions performed by these corrupt rulers and disassociate from their actions entirely and show people the true form of Islam as taught by our Prophet Muhammad (*sawa*) and his Household. It is up to us as God-fearing people to bridge the gaps between the two religions of Christianity and Islam; and to treat one another kindly with the aim to please the one and only God who created us all.

Imam Ali (*as*) is reported as saying *"Know that people are of two types: they are either your brothers in religion or your equal in creation."*

Find in-depth narrations of these stories and more in the book, *Christians who Defended and Died for Prophet Muhammad and his Family*, by Mateen J. Charbonneau, available at Amazon.

www.mateenjc.com

Made in the USA
Lexington, KY
07 October 2015